HOW TO CHOOSE THE RIGHT YACHT

J Muhs

ADLARD COLES NAUTICAL
London

This edition published 1994 by Adlard Coles Nautical
an imprint of A & C Black (Publishers) Ltd
35 Bedford Row, London WC1R 4JH

Copyright © Klasing & Co GmbH, Bielefeld 1991
Copyright © English language text
Adlard Coles Nautical 1994

ISBN 0-7136-3950-4

A CIP catalogue record for this book is available from the
British Library.

Translated by Petra Rattue from the German edition, *Wie
beurteile ich eine Yacht*
Edited by J C Winters

Typeset in 10/12pt Century by Falcon Graphic Art, Wallington,
Surrey.

Printed and bound in Great Britain by The Cromwell Press,
Melksham, Wiltshire

Contents

Preface

The first priority when buying a yacht is to decide just what your requirements are – and thus your expectations of what, after all, will probably turn out to be a very large financial investment. Are you planning a circumnavigation or do you prefer coastal cruising? Do you intend to race competitively occasionally, or not under any circumstances whatsoever? And (a decisive factor this, secondary perhaps only to that of price) do you have access to deep-water moorings or will the boat have to dry out between tides (for which either shoal or variable draft will be needed)? Once these matters have been settled – and they are bound to restrict the choice somewhat – it is clearly important to select the very best yacht available. However, because there are literally scores of designs on offer in each category or size range, many comparisons will have to be made before you can make your choice. Since boats that are superficially very similar can differ markedly in both performance and handling characteristics, this is not necessarily as straightforward as it might seem.

Advantages and disadvantages are not easy to weigh up simply by looking at each yacht, for there are numerous subtle aspects of design that distinguish an excellent product from one that is merely average. Admittedly, experience will make it easier to identify, with a degree of certainty, a boat that will be unmanageable or sluggish, but this evaluation process is rarely as instinctive as the intending buyer might be led to believe. An 'eye for a yacht' is not an innate characteristic; it is a skill that has to be acquired. Of course, most (if not all) intending purchasers will have read at least something of yacht design and the effect upon performance and seakindliness: magazine articles, test reports (even sales literature) are usually both interesting and informative. However, there are instances where such publications reveal more about the skills of journalist, copywriter and art editor than the skills of designer and boatbuilder. With sophisticated photographic techniques and wide-angle lenses (and also, dare it be said, a little judicious use of the air-brush), even the camera can lie!

Although looking over craft at boat shows is an enjoyable way to pass the time, it may not be much help when it comes to physical comparisons: the deck, cockpit and cabin will probably be besieged by crowds of like-minded members of the boating fraternity, and any view of the external hull will be obstructed by steps, placards and banks of flowers. At many boat shows, the craft will actually be afloat, so that the shape and section of the underbody can only be deduced from the manufacturer's brochure. And should you, as a matter of interest, take a pair of dividers to check the drawings and accommodation plans, you will probably note that the scale in the brochures is often 'stretched' – and that's putting it mildly! Even where there is ample opportunity to examine the boat in detail, unless you first have a clear idea of the way in which design affects the yacht's qualities, then even detailed inspection will tell you less about potential performance, manoeuvrability and seakindliness than it will about the standard of workmanship. To some extent, those in the business of selling boats count upon this lack of informed opinion in the same way as they rely upon the positive effects of a dazzling gelcoat or the mellow finish of the internal joinery.

So just how do you make an informed decision? Well, a yacht that is the offspring of a reputable designer and experienced builder obviously has a head start, but the qualities of a yacht are to some extent dependent upon the individual viewpoint: what one person regards as utter luxury is another's idea of purgatory afloat; what to one is a fast and responsive boat, feather light on the helm, will to another seem hypersensitive and unduly tender – and so on. Comments from those with boats of the same class are worth listening to, but in the end your decision must be based on your judgement and your judgement alone.

It should be borne in mind that, with the possible exception of dedicated racing boats, all designs are inevitably subject to a degree of compromise – a trade-off between simplicity and maximum efficiency, pure speed and the capability of sitting out heavy weather in relative comfort, knife-edge windward performance with moderate draft – and, all too often, a choice between adequate accommodation and aesthetic appeal.

There is obviously an intuitive element to the best designs, so there is no guaranteed formula either for the final assessment of a yacht. (Neither can a computer produce one with precise data and statistical values.) However, there *are* certain constants, and these can be used singly and together to form the basis of a fairly accurate calculated basis for valid comparison. From these constants, the yacht's performance can, to a large extent, be predicted through a defined range of wind and sea conditions and points of sailing. The information in this book should help you to examine a yacht from a practical viewpoint (even without setting foot on the craft), and the performance data – which is quite easy to work out – ought to go a long way in helping you choose the boat that is best for you.

1 The yacht itself

If there is one main criticism of modern glassfibre yachts, it is that their appearance tends to be starkly uniform. However, it can equally be argued that the boatbuying public has got exactly what it demanded: an emphasis on domestic niceties. These include double berths, galleys with all the trimmings of double sink, fridge and cooker and, since the design of yacht interiors mimics housing trends, not one WC but *two* (one en suite!). The boat is also required to look good. These are onerous demands to place upon a yacht that will be expected to sail and motor efficiently, manoeuvre predictably,

Sailing on a cruising yacht. This boat already shows signs of uncontrolled movements in a force 5. Is it because of its steep transom in association with a too-wide stern?

and be rewarding to handle. In addition, the overloaded beast must not only be self-righting, but unsinkable into the bargain! It is a lot to ask, and unfortunately most of these requirements are mutually incompatible.

The lack of individuality of hull, superstructure and rig is further reinforced by the fact that many craft share the same colour scheme: white with a mid-blue trim band. This being the case, it is not difficult to understand why potential buyers are persuaded that in fact the only real difference between the boats is the overall length of the hull. This is a fallacy – though in all fairness, all fibreglass production boats, by the very nature of construction method, do differ from one another less obviously than was the case when each boat was built on a one-off basis (usually to order – and in timber).

Because of the superficial resemblance between yachts, it has become especially important to make direct comparisons if specific qualities are to be recognised. The best (and most pleasant) way of establishing behavioural differences in designs is simply to sail several different examples in the size and price range you have in mind. However, in order to gain a true picture, each would have to be sailed in a wide range of wind strengths and sea states; this would rarely be feasible without the expense of a week's charter – and in any case, comparable boats may be lying hundreds of miles apart from one another.

However, as this book shows, there is another solution: no matter where the boats in question are based, it is possible to work out a theoretical comparison by calculations that use certain measurements of the boats. There will be some limitations – and there may also be discrepancies between the designer's measurements and *actual* measurements – but the theory works well in practice and could save you the wasted time, effort and expense of travelling around to inspect unsuitable yachts.

The facts

In the case of a cruising yacht, the requirements must be that it performs well on all points of sailing, remains controllable in all circumstances, and offers comfortable accommodation that is tenable offshore as well as in port. The vessel must, of course, be strongly constructed and practically equipped to cope with heavy weather. Of course, size has to be taken into account, and clearly a boat of 6 metres will not offer the comforts to be expected on a vessel twice that length; the differences in accommodation, deck and cockpit space imposed by size, though, are not too hard to assess by eye, whereas the sailing-handling qualities probably will be. Even the experienced may benefit from studying the comparison figures resulting from the use of calculations and coefficients. With practice, there comes a better awareness of hull shapes and associated characteristics.

When looking at a yacht, the first things likely to come to your attention are the overall length (and, possibly, the displacement), the keel and rudder, and the shape of the stem and stern. Also, you may get a general impression of the section and profile of the underbody. Don't be too dismissive at this stage; it is said that all cruising yachts are a compromise and appearances may be deceptive – that 'bathtub' you are looking at might turn in surprising speeds in certain conditions and be beautifully balanced as well.

Of course, each boat must be looked at in context – it is pointless to sneer at a motorsailer for possessing every conceivable onboard luxury if your own inclination is towards sheer, brutal performance at any price. Neither, by the same token, should you be unduly critical of a dedicated IOR-racer simply because the crew have to rough it in pipe cots!

Regrettably, the way in which boats are actually sold can be misleading: craft with an unrealistic number of berths and domestic utilities crammed in are portrayed as being fast enough to race – if not at the top level, then at least with a fair degree of success and, baldly, this concept of cruiser/racer does not work well with today's designs (racer/cruiser is, by definition, a combination with even less going for it!).

Sailing performance

Unfortunately, a yacht's performance is usually judged solely by the speed and the degree of ease with which other yachts can be outsailed. Top speeds of conventional ballasted yachts can hardly be improved upon because the speed is determined by the length of the waterline. As soon as it achieves its hull speed, every displacement yacht reaches a kind of barrier that cannot be broken, even if the sail area is increased.

This barrier can possibly be delayed by applying suitable constructive measures. A yacht's drive through the water is reduced because of resistances that every designer tries to keep to a minimum. His ability to do this is, however, limited because of clients' demands for certain measures and build features. (You can observe how well the designer has solved this task by observing the pull of the anchorline of a yacht anchored in a current; this is where friction and form resistance are unified into an overall hydrodynamic resistance that has to be overcome by the sail force.) The resistance due to friction on the underwater parts of a boat (skin friction) and the resistance due to the yacht's hull shape (form resistance) change with the speed of the water.

A slow sailing vessel may initially have to overcome more skin friction, but when it sails faster, then form resistance increases! The resistance due to friction also increases with the size of area that is submerged in the water – the wetted surface. A boat designer can influence the wetted surface by reducing the underwater hull, shortening the keel, and designing a sharper midship section. Another speed-reducing factor is the roughness of the hull. This is something that the boatyard will take care of initially, but it is, of course, the owner's responsibility to keep the bottom of his yacht clean in the future!

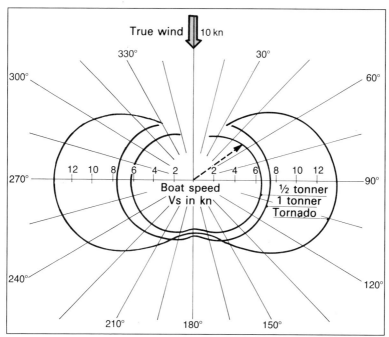

Fig 1 This diagram displays the measured speeds of three different yachts on different courses at a wind speed of 10 kn. While the drive of the 1/2 tonner and 1 tonner is mainly determined by their water-line length, the Tornado, being a catamaran, achieves extremely high speeds – mainly due to its low form resistance.

Displacement

The wave resistance of a displacement yacht also limits speed. This resistance eventually increases to such an extent that even increased drive power will only produce waves. The production of waves follows a physical rule whereby no energy is lost; it is simply transformed into a different form. When the particles of water reach the yacht, irrespective of whether the water is moving or the boat, they possess a certain velocity. The water particles are stopped at the hull; this decreases their movement or kinetic energy. Because the overall energy remains, comprising kinetic and potential energy (lifting energy), the potential energy has to increase, thus the water rises at the bow.

The kinetic energy increases again behind the sternpost, which increases the speed of the water particles – thus the water falls (away from sections where the hull is broadest). A wave trough develops, which becomes larger the higher the speed and the bigger the submerged volume. The trough stretches with increased speed and the wave moves further aft. A large displacement midships and a deep midship section that is U- or even V-shaped produce a deeper wave trough than light displacement with flat sections. Slim, well-drawn-out counters, as were once common in conventional long-keeled boats, produce the mount of the wave precisely at the end of their waterline.

In the search for speed, a yacht is affected by form resis-

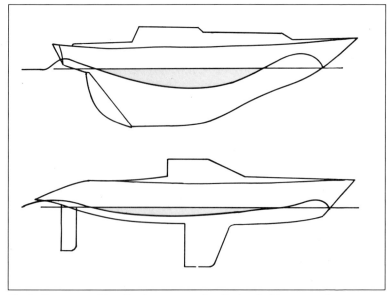

Fig 2 Because of its displacement, the fin-keeled boat produces a shallower wave pattern. It therefore achieves its hull speed faster, and might even exceed it if flat lines enlarge its wave-producing length.

tance; this is largely determined by the length of the hull, the fineness (or otherwise) of the ends and by the midship section. Together these combine to produce wave resistance, and this the designer can modify by alterations in the section and lengthening and fining the waterlines of the entry and run aft.

As well as these resistances, there is also the induced resistance of the hull, and this particular speed impediment is brought about by such factors as turbulence at the propeller, shaft bracket and rudder. A poorly designed transom is another common cause (or a transom that is too deeply immersed because there is excess weight carried aft). Steep heeling angles increase resistance markedly – especially in the case of those yachts with broad-beamed underbodies, and these should always be sailed upright. Windage caused by high freeboard, bulky superstructures and heavy masts with rigging to match – also, external halyards – has been claimed to add as much as 10 per cent to the overall adverse resistances.

This can be seen in some wooden boats. Yachts with overhanging and simultaneously flatter stern lines sometimes produce the wave crest behind the transom. If a yacht is sailing at or near ultimate speed, the bow and stern both lie on a wave crest. At this point a displacement yacht has reached the hull speed. In theory, it cannot get any faster because the aft wave will move so far astern that the bows will crash into a trough and the boat therefore has to sail more or less 'uphill'.

If the hull shape is cleverly designed, it might be possible to slightly expand the so-called 'wave-generating length', so that a light boat with only a few wave-producing lines can sail faster than its hull length in the water would actually permit. A shallow wave system requires less energy than a deeper one with the same wave length – therefore a yacht generating less waves also loses less energy for her drive.

Hull speed

Every wave has a speed that strictly depends on its length. It cannot move faster than $2.43\sqrt{\text{wave length}}$. Consequently, a

The wave crest at the bow and astern indicates that this Admiral's Cup yacht has reached hull speed. Extremely light displacement yachts are capable of reaching speeds up to $V_S \sqrt{\text{LWL}} = 3.62$.

displacement yacht that cannot produce a longer wave than its effective waterline permits is trapped in its own wave system and can only sail as fast as the wave; thus the ultimate speed is $2.43\sqrt{\text{LWL}}$ (speed in knots and length in metres).

Yachts with modern stern profiles may exceed this speed up to a value of 2.72 if the conditions are favourable; light displacement yachts might even reach speeds of up to $3.62\sqrt{\text{LWL}}$. To be precise, it depends on the effective wave-generating waterline, which can theoretically already be extended either through the boat heeling or by shifting the ballast. This produces the higher values.

Only racing machines, dinghies and light centreboarders can achieve true planing conditions. The speed of a Flying Dutchman (FD, 20ft International dinghy class), for example, has been measured at 14.5 knots, which results in a speed-to-length ratio of 6.34. A cruising yacht with full tanks and holiday gear will not be able to exceed the value of 2.43.

Fig 3 Ratios of stability on a sailing yacht: The heeling momentum (Wind pressure: Heeling force) and buoyancy momentum (Buoyancy: Righting force) are counterbalanced. Increasing wind pressure is counterbalanced by the righting force, which has become greater through stronger heeling.

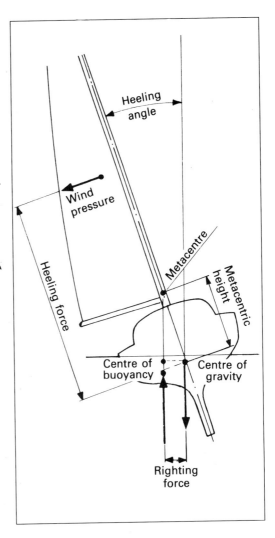

9

Stability

A sailing yacht will only attain ultimate speed if it is in a position to carry the necessary sail area for forward drive. The stability factor plays a vital role in the driving performance. The stability of a yacht is characterised by the ability to return upright from a heeled position. Sufficient stability is also, therefore, a safety factor.

Boats with ballast in their keels should consequently be unable to capsize, ie they should return to the upright position from any situation. A measure of stability is the metacentric height (GM or MG); this is equal to the distance between the yacht's centre of gravity G (the intersection of the effective line of buoyancy to the heeled central axis of the boat) and the metacentre (M).

For simplification, the centre of gravity (G) and the centre of buoyancy (B) are theoretical points that comprise all weights and all buoyancy. When the boat is upright, these points are on a theoretical vertical line. If the boat heels, the centre of buoyancy moves to leeward and produces the uprighting momentum with lever h (the line GB). A yacht's stability is therefore dependent on the position of both centres in relation to one another. The stability is made up from the form stability that derives from the hull shape, and the buoyancy stability that depends on the amount of ballast and its position. Modern displacement yachts generally have their ballast positioned so low that they return upright from heeling angles of up to 130 degrees – or more. These boats get stability primarily from a

Fig 4 (Opposite) Overall stability is produced from the sum total of the form stability: the wider the boat is, the greater is the form stability and the larger is the buoyancy stability. The larger the ballast weight and the lower its position, the larger will be the stability. Therefore, the stability is equal on both of the different boats shown in the diagram. M = metacentre; G = centre of gravity; B = centre of buoyancy (which invokes the uprighting). The comparison also shows that a good form stability offers a drier sail; while boat 1 already has her gunwales underwater, boat 2 still shows sufficient freeboard to leeward.

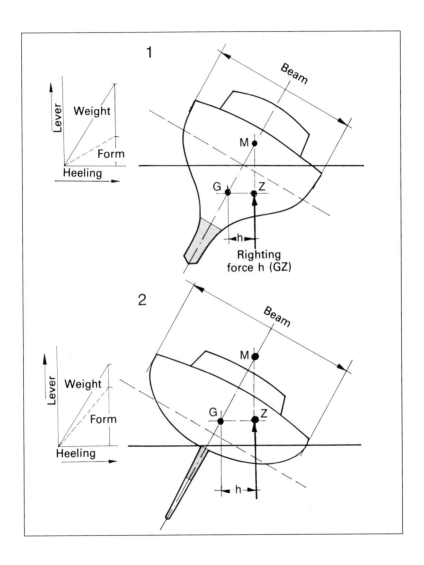

1

Lever
Weight
Form
Heeling

Beam
M
G • • Z
← h →
Righting
force h (GZ)

2

Lever
Weight
Form
Heeling

Beam
M
G • • Z
← h →

low centre of gravity (large amount of ballast or ballast sited low down in the keel) and the hull shape is secondary.

A wide-beamed hull, with high freeboard (as most modern yachts are built to provide superior accommodation), has a buoyancy gravity that moves far leeward when heeled and so contributes to the stability. This is why wide-beamed boats with high initial stability are known as 'form stable', and narrow-beamed boats that receive most of their stability from the weight of the ballast are known as 'buoyancy stable'. Despite this, form stability and buoyancy stability always go hand in hand. A slim yacht will always heel more, and consequently cut more smoothly into a rough sea. A wide-beamed boat generally sails much harder and faster at sea and might even provoke seasickness – but the sailing is that much drier.

A boat should therefore only be as wide beamed as required for stability. A good design is apparent from its counterbalanced form and buoyancy-stability. Designers have probably put more emphasis on the form stability for coastal cruisers that want to make port every night, while the oceangoing yacht will be equipped with more buoyancy stability so that crew and gear will not be stretched too far. Every yacht has to be designed with sufficient stability to enable the sail area required to reach the hull speed to be carried in a force 4 without having to reef.

The designer predetermines a yacht's characteristics, but you as a buyer should be able to form your own opinion of a boat by looking at its data and build characteristics. This way, you will be able to find the yacht that is best suited to your requirements.

2 Cruiser or dinghy?

Before looking seriously at sailing yachts, you should know which type of boat you are assessing. To define a sailing yacht and assign it into some sort of class is quite difficult. Although there is a large variety of boats on offer, you will not find a 'production-line boatyard' that wants to be placed into one particular category. These days, one can hardly tell the difference between racing yachts and cruiser/racers. This is one reason why cruiser/racers remain popular, although they are indefinable mixtures that are no good for either purpose.

With boats, you have to make similar differentiations to those you would make when choosing a car: between a runaround, everyday or luxury car. In the same way, you can only evaluate a boat correctly when you have determined whether it is a centreboarder or keel boat, coastal cruiser or ocean cruiser. There are specific criteria for each type of boat. For a yacht that does most of its sailing in a sunny climate, the cockpit cannot be too large, while the ocean cruiser's cockpit should be small for safety reasons (ideally less than 6 per cent of the yacht's volume).

Similar factors apply to many other areas: double berths, for example, are wonderful for boats that are moored up in harbour every night, but they are useless on ocean cruisers. A racing yacht has adjustable backstays in order to achieve good mast tuning, but on a cruising yacht these complicate the sailing. Every boat must therefore be classified. A starting criterion can be the boat's type, purpose and sailing area, and from there you can advance to further characteristics. You have to know the purpose for which the boat has been designed, and this question can best be answered by the designer. After all, he designed the boat for a specific purpose.

Although formal classification has not yet been introduced in Britain – and it is not certain quite how it will affect yachts (as opposed to commercial vessels and workboats) – it seems likely that yachts will be divided into categories:

Stability characteristics of boats tend to be linked to size: while the small cruiser (right) could not effectively set more sail on a reach, the larger yacht (below) can happily set a spinnaker on the same point of sailing and wind speed. Of course, very small boats have undertaken extensive voyages – in experienced hands – though this is perhaps not to be recommended. Although even these smaller craft are unlikely to capsize since the

majority have sufficient righting ballast, they may be at risk when offshore because of inadequate fittings, and dangerously large hatches and cockpit lockers. It must always be remembered, too, that because of the short waterline length, the course is easily deflected by wave action, and the hull speed will be necessarily low – probably too low for the boat to outrun approaching severe weather.

- Sailing dinghies
- Cruising dinghies
- Keelboats (without accommodation)
- Sailing yachts with accommodation
- Motorsailers

There is also some argument as to permitted cruising areas, and fittings and equipment required; and also possibly the most worrying point the question of enforcement. However, at present it is probably fair to say that with very few exceptions, most boats are suitable for the purpose stated by the manufacturer; it is mainly in the matter of details such as hatches, windows, deck equipment and ground tackle that anomalies occur. With an older yacht, it would be advisable to consult a surveyor.

3 What you read in the brochure

The boat's measurements define its characteristics: those most easily obtained are the overall length, the beam and the draught. However, the creature is more complex than this: waterline length, displacement and sail area are also specific values, which together form the overall picture.

Length

Surprising though it might seem, the actual overall length of a boat may differ from that given in the manufacturer's data (and occasionally even from that specified by the designer). The length overall can (and when quoted in brochures, frequently does) include bow platforms, pulpits, pushpits, boarding ladders and davits – even transom hung rudders! This length, though, is defined as the total length, and should not be confused with the overall length upon which calculations such as the enclosed area or volume are made. (Pragmatically though, it is the *total* length upon which the harbour or marina fees will be levied!) The waterline length is also important, as this will be needed in order to work out the boat's maximum theoretical hull speed.

Length overall (LOA)

The length overall is taken as the distance from the trailing edge of the transom to the extreme forward edge of the stem. It is measured parallel to the flotation line and excludes any projecting deck fittings. It is always the length of the hull *only*, and this definition is used by boatbuilders and designers. A 10-metre boat should be just that – 10 metres – so if there is any doubt, measure it!

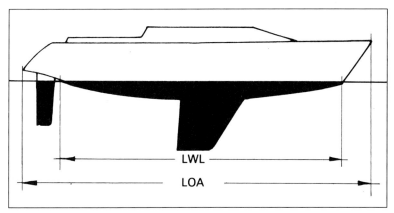

Fig 5 The length is one of the main measurements of a yacht. The length of the waterline (LWL) is responsible for the yacht's speed. LOA describes the hull without such fittings as pulpits, etc.

Waterline length (LWL)

The waterline length is measured at the fore-and-aft ends of the flotation line. The datum (or designed) and actual load waterline lengths frequently differ slightly, but it is the actual load waterline that determines the hull speed in a displacement hull.

Breadth

A boat's beam is divided in the same way as its length is: breadth overall and breadth on the waterline. A boat's breadth gives stability; the beamier the boat, the better is the form stability. Having said this, the breadth also acts as a brake, and designers are therefore concerned with keeping the breadth on the waterline to a minimum.

The cross-section of the boat's widest part is called 'midship section'. In vessels with harmonic all round qualities, it can be found in the middle of the waterline length (0.5 LWL); in small cruisers with wide sterns it is often found in the aft third. This has the disadvantage of giving the boat a lot of weatherhelm when heeled.

Breadth overall (BOA)

The breadth overall defines the largest breadth of the hull, measured from the outer edge of the outer hull, exclusive of rubbing strakes. This measurement, in connection with the hull length, permits assumptions about the enclosed area (volume): the beamier the hull, the more space is below deck.

Breadth in the waterline (BWL)

The breadth in the waterline is the breadth of a boat that is ready equipped for sailing, measured on the flotation line. If multiplied with the LWL, it produces a waterline-triangle. This is the basis for calculations with regard to the sail-carrying ability of fin-keeler, bilge-keeler and centreboarders. The BWL is responsible for a boat's initial stability.

Draught

The draught is defined as the vertical distance between the flotation line of a boat equipped ready for sailing and the lower edge of the keel. It contributes to the enlargement of the lateral plan, but hardly at all to the initial stability (stiffness). The draught only produces more buoyancy stability when the boat is heeled sufficiently, ie when the ballast becomes effective.

Freeboard

In open boats, the freeboard is the smallest distance between the boat's flotation line and the upper edge of the gunwale. In craft with a deck it will be measured up to the upper edge of the deck at its lowest part. If a boat's heeling angle is fairly low, a high freeboard reduces the stability, because a hull that

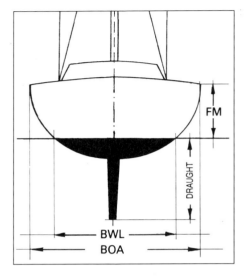

Fig 6 The breadth on the waterline (BWL) represents stability and form resistance. Freeboard (FM) and breadth overall (BOA) increase the stability when the boat is heeling more.

emerges high above the surface of the water also lifts its centre of gravity. The stability increases again through greater buoyancy of the hull, if the heeling is further increased. This becomes especially evident in boats with wide-beamed sections, which have a greater immersed volume when heeled.

Displacement as a weight

A yacht's displacement weight is the weight equipped for sailing. This weight comprises the dead load, the hull with its fixed parts of equipment, and the extra load. The extra load is the sum total of the persons permitted (approximately 75 kilograms), tank contents, safety equipment, sails, personal gear (up to a maximum of 30 kilograms per crew member) and provisions. Outboard engines and fuel cans are also included in the extra load. Boats are divided into heavy, medium and light displacement. Another term that is common among racing people is 'ultralight' – which is pretty much self-explanatory!

Displacement as a volume

The displacement in the water describes the volume of a yacht that is equipped ready for sailing, up to the submerged flotation line. It is the quotient from displacement (D) and density of the displaced water (density of sea water = 0.975). Boatyards often advertise a yacht's displacement in their brochures, but it generally means the deadweight of the boat without equipment. (If you want to trail your boat, you *must* know its deadweight *and* the tow capacity of your car! Beware though – manufacturers' estimated weights are notoriously inaccurate. If in doubt, head for a public weighbridge to check.)

Ballast

The ballast describes the part of the displacement that contributes to the (weight) stability as either external ballast (contained in the keel (or keels)) or internal ballast (within the boat). It enables a boat to carry sails. The most common ballast is lead or cast-iron, and for a cruising boat the weight should be between 40 and 50 per cent.

Sail area

When comparing sail areas you will generally find the close-hauled sail plan stated: on masthead rigs this is the sum total of mainsail and 150 per cent genoa. This represents a fair definition for the narrow mainsail and enormous foresails. It also enables a comparison between masthead-rigged and fractional-rigged (7/8-rig) yachts. For this, you calculate the main and the largest foresail without overlap, which is generally the no 1 jib.

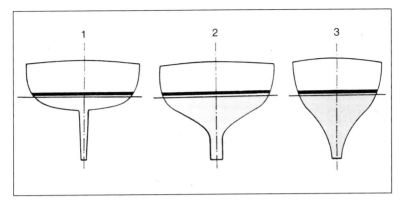

Fig 7 A yacht's midship section displays the displacement. A low displacement only requires a small volume in the water and allows flatter lines (**1**); high displacement is always associated with a higher volume (**2** and **3**).

4 The yacht's qualities

To the majority of intending boatowners, the performance of the yacht will be of prime importance; although a boat cannot be assessed in precisely the same way as a car, its behaviour is similarly the result of a number of components designed to work together in harmony. As with a car, your requirements must be clearly set out in your own mind; and (as with cars) there will be certain compromises that must be accepted.

In the case of a sailing boat, such compromises will tend to lead you towards a particular type of yacht: perhaps a motor-sailer whose performance under sail alone is secondary to onboard comfort and economy and ease of handling under power; or possibly a fine lined yacht – one that inclines to be tender, but that points high and sails fast (though in so doing, will give the crew a wet ride); or, a third option, the maligned 'floating caravan' – this will have above average accommodation for the overall length. This latter option may require a bit of determination by the skipper to persuade the vessel to reach the maximum hull speed, but (though it may tend to slam into head seas) it will, nevertheless, prove quite stiff and dry.

A good deal does depend on your cruising area: if most of your sailing is in the Baltic (in summer, that is!) or in the Mediterranean, lighter construction would be acceptable – and a large cockpit and generous sail plan would be handy. However, if sailing in exposed waters, the boat must be strong, the cockpit small and well protected, and the vessel able to keep to the sea in a gale if necessary. It must also point well enough to windward to be able to claw off a dangerous lee shore. The rig should be easily handled and all the deck hard-ware must be to the highest possible specification. In tidal rivers and estuaries, the ability to short tack quickly is a real asset, as is a hull form that does not lose way in a short, steep sea. (Shallow or variable draught is often useful in these areas, too!)

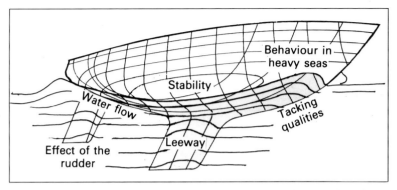

Fig 8 A variety of factors contribute to a boat's quality: a pointed deep bow offers good tacking qualities and flat underwater lines allow a free water flow at the stern. A profiled fin keel produces the lateral stability required to sail a boat; a full midship section gives sufficient form stability. Unfortunately, it is not possible to combine all positive design features into one hull, so that each design remains a compromise with its own special qualities depending on the owner's requirements or cruising area.

Of course, there are some qualities that every yacht should have: the ability to tack clear of a lee shore if an onshore wind threatens to push you on to the coast, and sufficient stability for righting even from extreme heeling angles.

Fast sailing

A yacht's speed depends primarily on wind force and sail area. We are now talking about qualities that the designer selected in order to make the boat comparatively fast.

The factors that influence a boat's speed are various. The brochure may already present some factors that can be derived from a boat's measurements and used for later calculation:

The **length of the waterline**: The longer the LWL, the higher the maximum speed (see definition of hull speed).

Displacement: The lower the displacement, the flatter can be the hull shape and lines, and it requires less wind to bring

23

the boat up to hull speed. The relationship of the displacement towards the waterline indicates the wave-producing length and also shows whether a boat is light or heavy.

The **wetted surface**: Defines the area that is submerged in the water and can roughly be estimated from the vessel's length, beam and draught. A yacht will sail faster in light winds, given a lower wetted surface. In stronger winds, the proportion of the friction resistances (see page 4) decreases from the overall resistance, thus it outweighs the wave resistance. Narrow, deep fin-keelers only have a small submerged surface, and are therefore good in light winds.

The next two factors cannot be obtained from the brochure. They need to be calculated; this will be explained in a later chapter, but is worth mentioning at this point in order to complete the list:

The **stability** is a function of sail area, displacement and breadth on the waterline. The higher the stability, the more sail area can be carried and the faster the boat will sail. The yacht's sail-carrying ability therefore derives from the relationship between sail area and displacement.

The **cylinder coefficient** will be explained in the Appendix (p. 116), but it also needs mentioning here as there are some boat dealers who boast of it. It is a measure of the distribution of a yacht's submerged volume across the hull length. The higher this coefficient is, the more wind is required for a yacht to reach the hull speed.

If you are looking for a cruiser, you should put a lot of emphasis on the length of the waterline and stability, but less on a lower cylinder coefficient – which only makes the yacht more tender. A comfortable but heavier interior layout with an additional 50 kilogram ballast is usually more important for a pleasant sail that 50 kilogram placed in the keel, where it would increase the boat's stability and allow it to carry more sail.

Boatyards are aware of this, and in most cases only build the first boat of a series fast (minimal interior layout, no equipment). The weights stated in the brochure are subsequently only correct for this one particular vessel. Only a

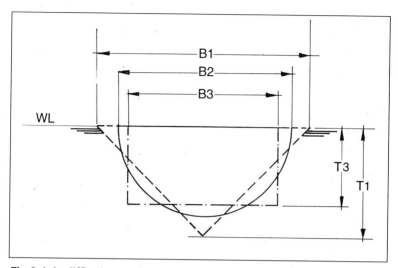

Fig 9 It is difficult to estimate a yacht's submerged surface. These three idealised hull shapes offer a rough idea; the semi-circle (with equal displacement) has therefore got the lowest wetted surface, while the triangle's and the rectangle's submerged surface is nearly 13 per cent higher. Hence, the U-shape of most fin-keeled boats is less submerged than the wide rectangle of a light bilge-keeler. The rectangular shape also has the smallest breadth (B3) and the shortest draught (T3). The rounded shape with medium measures for beam and draught would be ideal. The triangle has the largest draught (T1).

yacht that is empty will float on the designed waterline. If you buy the version with two WCs, aft cabin and fully equipped galley, your boat would lie 4 centimetres deeper in the water and consequently not perform as stated. This is why you should be very cautious of so-called cruiser/racers.

Sailing to windward

The height to the true wind is defined as the angle that a yacht can sail to windward. In practice, it is the tacking arc measured at the true wind divided by two. Statistics show that a yacht only sails close-hauled for a quarter of her time (though it doesn't always seem so!). Sailing to windward is nevertheless an important criterion, and one in which rigging and sails also play a part. A cruising yacht cannot generally sail closer than 40 degrees to the true wind, which means sailing nearly a third of the way farther than a motor boat driving directly into the wind. Out at sea, though, the ability to sail close-hauled is not that vital, and it is more important for a yacht to perform well on a beam reach. When tacking in narrow channels or rivers, though, every metre, clawed up to the wind, really counts! Although the expected height to windward depends strongly on the hull's hydrofoilic qualities, it is a combined effort of hull and sails.

The narrower a boat is, the higher it can point to windward. The origin of this opinion derives from the relatively heavy long-keelers, which have a large lateral area in the water and subsequently make less leeway than a beamy hull. Hydrofoilic qualities are also known as lateral buoyancy. A good lateral buoyancy, thus good lateral force, represents smaller drifting angles, ie less leeway.

Despite this, there are wide-beamed full hulls that can point just as high, or even higher, than a narrow boat – so long, that is, as they are sailed upright and with caution. These hulls obtain their lateral buoyancy from a profiled fin keel and equivalent fin rudder (these are so-called NACA-profiles that originate from tank testing and are especially suitable as yacht keels). The following rule applies for these fins (or hydrofoils): the higher their aspect ratio – ie the longer and narrower the hydrofoil (fin) is and therefore the larger the draught – the smaller is their drifting angle. A well-sailed yacht can point up to 34 degrees to windward with these fins. One condition that is necessary to obtain such high pointing is a clean water flow at the fin, which requires a smooth transition to the hull (flat bottom) and an often bulged lower edge of the keel (or even a winged keel) as a so-called 'end plate'. The effect of this is to prevent the flow at the end from drifting away. These boats, though, are more difficult to sail, are very

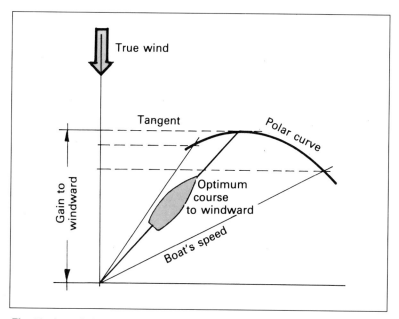

Fig 10 A yacht's pointing ability to windward is one criterion of its sailing performance. Even more important is the relation of the boat's speed to pointed height – the so-called 'gain to windward', which is the distance made good to windward. The tangent on the polar curve, to which the angle of the wind is projected, indicates the optimal course.

unforgiving of mistakes, and are generally not very course stable. The flow around narrow keels cuts off a lot earlier, so that finding the most efficient course is more difficult. This is why a boat with a narrow fin keel can only sail close to windward when it has sufficient drive: in lighter winds it becomes necessary to bear away more in order to keep way on. The following example displays what a good speed, together with good lateral height, means for sailing close to windward (ie for the ultimate course to windward). One should consider this prior to buying a yacht: the helmsman of a yacht has no reason to gloat over the dinghy helm because he is able to point 35 degrees to windward and the dinghy only points 45 degrees.

The yacht's route might only be 22 per cent longer than the direct direction into the wind, while the dinghy's route is 41 per cent longer; however, because of the speed, the dinghy will still reach its destination a lot faster – final speed to windward is higher. Speed and height to windward are therefore directly related to one another and cannot be separated. Important for a good performance to windward is therefore the boat's final speed to windward, generally described as $V_{windward}$, which should be as high as possible in each wind force. This angle is the product of speed and the cosine of course angle. The upper part of Fig 10 clarifies the relation of speed and course angle. It is therefore not worth your while aiming for a boat that can point extremely high; what you need is the optimal course with the better final speed to windward. It is therefore not vital for a cruiser to have an extremely narrow and deep fin; boats with a medium cut-away keel that have less draught, or even boats with a conventional long keel, will achieve good final speeds – and also have the advantage when approaching shallower harbours.

Manoeuvrability and course stability

Many sailors are convinced that to combine good manoeuvrability with acceptable directional stability is an impossibility. In the more extreme examples of fin-keeled racing boats, responsive to the slightest twitch of the rudder, this does hold true – such boats cannot be left to their own devices even for a moment. However, this type is not designed – or, equally important, constructed – with passage-making in mind. To take the other extreme, though, the 'traditional', directionally stable, long-keeled cruising boat (which admittedly takes its time in answering the helm) is not the only type of cruiser – nor, arguably, the best all-rounder.

The best all-rounders are generally yachts with medium fins, whose lines, if extended, would be like those of a long keel, but where a section aft has been cut away (cut-away keel). This is why one talks about an interrupted lateral plan in connection with these boats. A modern yacht that has such a fin keel (albeit of less extreme form than a racing yacht), with a skeg in front of the rudder, can be both stable and manoeuvrable.

The long, continuous lateral plan of a long keel is definitely less sensitive on the rudder because of its larger inertia. This makes it more suited to ocean cruises. However, for navigating narrow harbours and marinas, you need a boat that is easier to manoeuvre.

Looking at a long keel, you will find that it has a good deal of submerged surface – hence increased friction resistance. The connected braking effect will therefore be especially noticeable in light winds. (Narrow long-keelers with an S-section compensate for this by their lower proportion of wetted surface.) Thus yacht designers shortened the length of the keel, which led to the so-called 'interrupted' or 'divided lateral' profile. (Subsequent shortening led to the small fin keel with a large draught.)

If such a keel is to assist course stability it must possess a good keel-to-rudder alignment, so that the lateral force and the force of the rudder counterbalance the pressure of the sails, even at different heeling angles. Unfortunately, you will not be able to detect this at first glance. Cut-away keels are more suitable for cruisers, as they are more forgiving of errors – both those made by the designer and, later on, those made by the sailor!

Fin keels are not only effective by virtue of the size of the area, they obtain their required lateral force from the profile and thus need more speed through the water. A narrow fin also needs to be correspondingly thin, but there are limits because the attachment must be strong. The keel must also carry the required ballast. Extremely narrow fin-keelers are therefore not suitable as cruising yachts, since the crew must perch on the windward side; their advantage, though, is very good manoeuvrability. Since this is associated with a very sensitive helm, the tiller cannot be left unattended even for a brief moment, though.

1

2

The long lateral profile (**1**) of this 14 metre long-keeled yawl assures good directional stability; however, the length of the lateral profile also reduces – or, more accurately, *slows* – the manoeuvrability (and siting the rudder directly aft of the keel does not help either). The cut-away keel (**2**) with a skeg in front of the rudder is a good compromise, with the continuous transition from hull to keel (rather like the shape of a wineglass) still visible, but in **3**, a lighter displacement design, the hull becomes flatter in section and the keel is no longer part of the hull; it has become separate, although faired in slightly at the root. The rudder

3

4

has now been moved farther aft, but is hung to a full skeg. The underwater hull of this yacht (4) would be quite unacceptable for a cruiser; there is no skeg or heel bearing to the rudder (these can be clearly seen in 2 and 3), which is hung only on its stock and very vulnerable to damage. Both fin and rudder are now appendages, separate from the hull rather than integrated into it as in 1. The hulls of 3 and 4 bear a close resemblance to dinghy hulls and, like any dinghy, are extremely sensitive to the slightest helm movement.

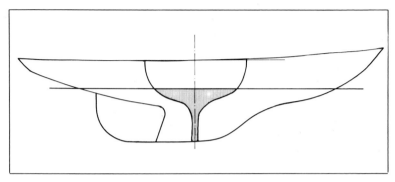

Fig 11 By shortening the lateral profile, which eventually resulted in fin keels, yachts became faster because of the reduction of the boat's wetted surface. Only the first third of the lateral profile is required to give the boat its lateral buoyancy, so that the section aft of that can be cut away (cut-away keeler). The aspect ratio, draught-to-width of the keel, increases, but the buoyancy remains equal.

A narrow fin-keeler can only regain its more user-friendly qualities if it has a skeg in front of the rudder that is about half of the profile area of the rudder blade itself, as well as a slim, deep bow. A long keel obtains its lateral force almost solely from the front half of the lateral plan. Behind that, this is so negligible that it can be dismissed, and so designers cut away this section in order to minimise the wetted surface.

Short-keelers can combine manoeuvrability and directional stability if designed properly, but keels that are particularly shallow have another disadvantage: the buoyancy of the fin is reduced drastically when going about at a low speed (it depends on the square of the speed). The boat loses way – and therefore the fin becomes less effective – if it is not driven with a sufficiently large angle of incidence. You can often observe these yachts drifting sideways in harbour as they attempt to gather speed.

This disadvantage is reduced by building deeper keels, because the lateral buoyancy also increases with the square of the draught. In contrast to this, though, are the desires of sailors to be able to enter any harbour: the draught of a cruising yacht should therefore not be allowed to exceed 1.6 metres. Extremely short keels tend to tilt on to their noses when dried out – and are also very sensitive to contact with solid ground! This results in a requirement for a cruising yacht that is as easy to manoeuvre as a fin-keeler, but at the same time directionally stable; and this can be a difficult compromise for the designer – and the buyer!

Stiffness

A 'stiff' boat is also a boat with good stability; but, despite this, stiffness should be defined differently. A stiff boat does not heel quickly in a gust of wind and hardly moves when somebody steps on to deck. Both of these factors seem positive at first glance, because they give a feeling of security. However, the question that should be asked is whether a tender boat (the reverse of stiff) does not have the better qualities at sea.

The stability of a boat comprises, as already mentioned, form stability and buoyancy stability, interpreted as the heeling angle up to the point of capsize. The stiffness depends mainly on the boat's initial – and therefore form – stability. This is because the ballast only becomes effective in heeling angles with sufficient leverage. At heeling angles of up to 30 degrees, the form stability determines the stiffness of a boat; with beamier boats, the stiffness is further increased with a correspondingly higher metacentre M above the water surface. The actual factor for the form stability is the shape of the hull. The beamier the sections, the more additional volume is brought into the water – thus the stiffer the boat. This quality, which was initially judged as positive, leads to uncomfortable behaviour at sea. The consequence of too much stiffness is jerky movements and smashing into waves, which is demanding upon both hull and crew.

Slim boats with a large amount of ballast might heel more quickly, but their deep hulls (more buoyancy stability) react more sluggishly. This makes them more comfortable for the crew at sea.

Wet or dry?

One desirable quality of a cruising boat is that it should, even when sailing hard, refrain from scooping up water and throwing it over the long-suffering crew! Whether or not it does this depends upon the stability and also the buoyancy at the bow and stern (which should be balanced to a large extent, for otherwise a pitching moment will be exaggerated). A narrow boat, with low initial stability, will heel sharply and put the gunwale under with great alacrity – although given a cockpit, well protected by high coamings, this may not bother the crew unduly; after all, not much in the way of solid water will actually reach them! (A yacht with a high freeboard will, naturally, have correspondingly less water on deck even at a high angle of heel.)

However, a good deal of the water that may come aboard is the direct result of the boat sailing fast and burying the bows in the waves; this is the result of a lack of buoyancy forward –

Yachts with insufficient buoyancy at the bow (acute V profiles) tend to undercut, as you can see in this photo. A wet sail is the result. It is recommended that boats like this are sailed with a smaller headsail.

and boats with a fine entry coupled with deeply vee'd sections forward are very prone to 'undercut', especially in a head sea. A certain amount of 'flare' – an outward curve to the topsides, so that the beam at the gunwale is greater than it is on the waterline – will tend to fling water clear, and also it increases the buoyancy forward as the vessel heels. It does, however, increase drag, since the deck edge, along with the toerail, stanchions, etc may be immersed as heeling increases. Sometimes a knuckle is moulded into the topsides to serve the same purpose (and also to stiffen the topsides of a GRP boat), but this hardly enhances the appearance – and, once again, can create additional resistance.

Simplistic though it is, the basics hold true: fast boats wet, slow boats dry! However, in strengthening winds, there will come a point when a beamy boat, sailing at maximum hull speed, will be as wet as any fine-lined boat – although high freeboard and superstructure may keep the crew more comfortable.

Seaworthiness

Every prospective buyer is entitled to expect his or her yacht to be safe at sea – in other words, to be seaworthy. How is seaworthiness defined, though?

Well, clearly, it is more than a matter of *hull* design: for a start, the yacht's construction must be strong and structurally in a sound state. The design of the cockpit must be carefully thought out: it must be large enough to seat the crew on watch, protect them so far as is possible from the elements, and allow them good all-round visibility; it should also (preferably) be self-draining. Windows and hatches must be watertight and, where necessary, capable of being secured against a capsize or total inversion (many 'cruising boats' have hatches and skylights that are insubstantial and far too large for safety). Deck fittings and ground tackle must be adequate for the size of the vessel and, of course, the rig must be strong, well supported and easy to handle under any circumstances. Such a boat should be able to withstand heavy weather and ought to be capable of making some progress to windward in all but the very worst conditions. It would be expected to remain controllable and to lie hove-to in a gale – hopefully, too, it should be blessed with an easy motion in a seaway, though there are some circumstances in which this might seem a bit over-optimistic! Needless to say, to be regarded as seaworthy, any yacht must also possess sufficient stability and righting ballast to recover from a knock-down.

A sound cruising yacht must also have a well-planned layout below; this does not mean accommodation that is crammed full with luxuries, but rather one that provides a fixed berth for each off-watch crew member, an efficient cooker (preferably fiddled and hung in gimbals), and enough space to use it safely (much the same goes for the WC, incidentally!). There should also be a stable chart table – preferably one that is large enough to spread out a complete chart.

Such qualities are a lot to expect from any boat, yet such working craft as sailing trawlers, the Bristol Pilot Cutters and the famous Colin Archer-designed rescue boats have all managed to combine them – and without the benefit of modern technology and computers! The design of these craft is not only functional, but also beautiful: not only above the waterline, but below as well – with soft sections merging into the long keel and well-balanced ends. (Well-balanced, in this context, means that the fullness of the underbody is amidships and the sections of bow and stern are reasonably (and this is important) similar to one another in volume.) Hulls undistorted by rating rules and free from the extremes of sawn-off transoms, snubbed bows and peculiar midships bulges represent the best of cruising boat design and are unlikely to exhaust the crew by violent motion in a seaway. Also, a hull with harmonious ends is less likely to develop lee or weather helm when heeled, and so should maintain a course easily – without tearing the helmsman's arm from its socket, or flattening the battery of the autopilot!

In comparison to boats like this, there are extreme racing boats whose hulls are very light and intended for speed and

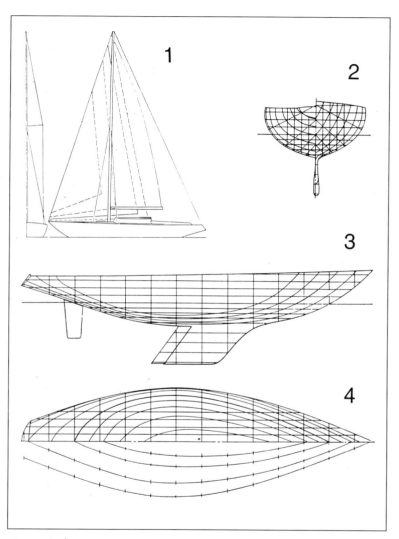

Fig 12 Sail plan (**1**), sections (**2**), profile (**3**) and waterline plan (**4**) of
Tina, who won the one-ton trophy in 1966. Her lines stand out with
harmonic simplicity. *Tina* sailed extremely comfortably, lay calmly
in the water, even in rough seas, and cut smoothly into the waves.

nothing but speed (though usually each is designed to perform optimally within a given range of wind strengths – few are outstanding all-rounders). All these types are very hard to control and cannot therefore be regarded as seaworthy – even when they are strongly constructed (which is rarely, if ever, the case).

With practice, you will be able to recognise a yacht whose shape is well balanced and harmonious. Of course, back in the days when most boats were constructed of wood, such was nearly always the case – indeed, the nature of the material itself forced designer and boatbuilder to produce vessels with sweetly flowing lines. Timber planks, after all, do not take kindly to distortion and it is all but impossible to build the type of form currently engendered by the rating rules in carvel or even clinker strakes (although it is possible with moulded veneer)!

However, along came computers – and high-tech boatbuilding – and sections and sterns sprouted bumps, blisters and bustles, all in order to improve the rating. The pity of it is that cruising boats followed suit for no logical reason other than fashion. Many of these boats, more or less directly derived from competitive craft, were (and are) designed without any consideration of the waters and wave systems in which they will sail. Neither are these boats pleasing to look at – and there's a lot of truth in the old maxim: if she looks right, she'll sail right!

In comparison to these boats, you find extreme designs for racing, whose hull shapes increase their sail area. They are fitted out with all possible features simply to increase speed. These boats are hard to control and therefore not seaworthy.

With a little bit of practice you will be able to recognise a boat with well-balanced lines: in the days of wooden yachts, these lines came naturally. Planks of wood bend in curves – and *only* in curves! These curves seem pleasant to look at because of their even and harmonious proportions. The flow of the water is harmonic too. A beautiful and well-balanced hull also sails well. To recognise the beauty of a boat's hull is part of its evaluation. Only when computers replaced the strake batten from the designer's drawing board were stern areas designed that bulged and had constrictions (apparently unnecessary dents in order to achieve a better rating for racing). This caused designers to create cruising yachts with extreme lines, often with a blatant neglect of the wave system in which the boat is supposed to sail. As already mentioned, the flow of the water follows the wooden strake battens. Such hull lines, ie the shape of these boats, are also extremely seaworthy.

Behaviour at sea

Wind and waves deal harshly with a boat: they accelerate it, slow it down, and cause it to dance on the water – and the rougher the sea and the smaller the boat, the worse it is! Unfortunately, not every boat can be built as large as an owner might wish: financial considerations and ease of handling are also limiting factors. However, there are design features that allow a smaller yacht to counteract these unpleasant movements – or at least not exaggerate them, eg a slightly higher displacement, well-balanced stability (and not too flat a hull shape).

The main oscillations of a boat in heavy seas are pitching, rolling and yawing. A boat is rolling when it moves from side to side along its length axis. (This is often supplemented with diving movements that further increase the angle of rolling.) The designer can restrain this by building a hull shape with more lateral buoyancy, as this counteracts the rolling to a certain extent.

A pitching boat moves rhythmically around the cross axis (up and down), which becomes worse the better it integrates into the wave system. A well-designed yacht can reduce the pitching by concentrating as much weight as possible around the centre of gravity and with a finer bow area that cuts more smoothly into the water.

Yawing is a rhythmic rolling movement around the vertical axis (around the mast, so to speak). Yawing subsequently leads to broaching. Good course stability reduces the yawing

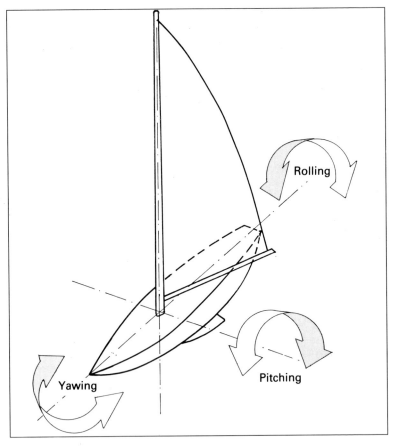

Fig 13 The three main oscillating movements in heavy seas are rolling, pitching and yawing. A seakindly boat should be able to minimise these movements. Pitching is reduced by concentrating weight around the boat's centre of gravity in association with well-balanced buoyancy astern. An evenly distributed righting moment on every heeling angle reduces rolling and a good keel-to-rudder alignment reduces yawing.

movement – for this you require good alliance between keel and rudder. Long-keeled yachts display a reduced tendency to yaw – short-keeled boats should therefore have a skeg. You should pay attention to these features if purchasing a cruising boat. A cruiser should be expected to reduce these three oscillating movements by using the slowest possible acceleration – it is the abrupt changes of speed that make a yacht unpleasant to sail. If these movements cannot be endured, the crew will not be able to sail the boat safely, let alone enjoy the sailing. Today's modern yachts, which are generally flat and bowl-shaped, are exposed to the forces of the sea because of their tendency to skitter along the surface of the water.

While earlier yachts had roughly two-thirds of their hull submerged in the water, the cruiser/racer concept seems today to favour the reverse. These boats might have become faster, but their rolling and pitching movements are so short and undiminished that the boat often accelerates far too fast. Under such circumstances, seasickness is likely even in light winds. The best cruising yacht is the one with the smoothest movements: these can only be found in yachts with harmonious hull shapes.

Accommodation

An additional safety aspect is a modicum of comfort aboard, because only a rested crew can sail safely over long periods. In comparison with racing yachts, cruising yacht interiors are generally fitted out with teak or mahogany. Most of these layouts are only practical when in harbour, and are unsuitable for sailing. They feature double bunks that are useless when the boat is heeling, galleys with ill-fitted attachments for the cooker – not to mention the seating spaces below deck whereby the crew sit on each other's laps even when still in harbour. The sailing performance also frequently suffers because of too much internal weight: two WCs, a shower, an over-sized cool-box (possibly a generator) and other shore comforts, none of which are strictly necessary. A limit should be placed on interior fittings, otherwise performance may be affected.

The ideal layout should be functional for passage-making and habitable in a harbour. When buying a yacht, you should choose the layout that fits your own personal requirements. It depends on the type of boat, but even mass-produced boats are subject to change – within limits, of course.

Some people are under the impression that the interior layout is designed by sailing people; unfortunately this is seldom the case. More often than not, functionality has to give way to more bunks, and boatyards reduce the bilge section in favour of sufficient headroom! By limiting the bunks to the number actually required, a sensible layout could be designed so that areas where headroom is required, ie galley, WC and passageways, can be placed where headroom is available: next to the companionway. Other concepts can be achieved through wider beam, cambered decks or even raised decks. Sitting headroom is sufficient above bunks and seats. Because of the lower hull depth of modern light constructions, the height of the freeboard has been increased, which is no disadvantage for larger boats as it raises the buoyancy. However, to try and create headroom on a 6-metre boat and then sell it as a cruising yacht is irresponsible. If you are thinking of purchasing a mini-cruiser, you should be sceptical.

Even on larger yachts, the interior layout can influence a boat's qualities. It is always a disadvantage if too much solid wood has been used for the interior as this only lifts the boat's centre of gravity. Extra attention should also be given to the fact that heavy bunks in the forepeak, and the nowadays common double bunks in the aft cabin, cause unnecessary pitching when underway; always remember that as much weight as possible should be concentrated around the boat's centre of gravity, ie in the middle.

Double bunks have become increasingly popular at boat shows. They might be very comfortable for the nights spent in harbour, but narrow bunks are required when underway so that the sleeper can be wedged in. Double bunks should only be tolerated in the forepeak, and even then they should be designed as light pipe cots. The forepeak is not generally ideal for sleeping underway because of loud noises and uncomfortable movements. All other bunks should be single bunks, which should be already made up (no lowering of tables and so on).

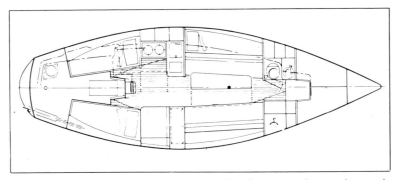

Fig 14 This interior design has proved itself on seagoing yachts and is preferred by real cruising yachtsmen. There are no double berths or dinette. Two quarter berths are positioned under the cockpit, two further ones in the saloon on the port and starboard side, and the common 'vee-berth' in the forepeak. The most important areas, navigation and galley, are built where the highest headroom is. Unfortunately, this means that the WC had to be placed between the saloon and the forepeak, although it is preferable to have it close to the companionway.

Most suitable for sailing yachts are pilot berths on the sides and quarter berths, although they should be easy to get in and out of!

Diagonal berths are totally unnautical as they are highly impracticable: when the boat is heeled, the occupant is either standing on their head or on their feet. If double berths cannot be avoided, they should be separated with a lee cloth. Even if you do not intend to set out in a gale, your boat should still be furnished sensibly. Whether the interior design is to your personal taste is often only determined after a holiday afloat. By looking at a few details, though, one can normally quickly establish whether the boat has been designed by sailors (handrails, fiddles, seagoing berths, etc). A good interior design contributes towards good sailing performance if it is of fairly light weight, and preferably placed around the centre of gravity.

Safety

When questioning the safety of a yacht, the thought upper-most in the mind is usually 'Will the craft capsize?' Hard on the heels of this, an intending purchaser might well ask, 'Will it sink?' With boats there are no absolutes, of course, but it is certainly possible to design and build a yacht that is, theoreti-cally, unsinkable. In the case of a light displacement boat, whether of timber or GRP, buoyancy tanks can be inbuilt, and it does not need much positive buoyancy to counteract the rel-atively small amount of ballast on such a craft. Given a dis-placement cruising boat with not only a ballast keel – perhaps accounting for just under half the total weight – and an engine, cooker and all the paraphernalia of passage-making, it can be seen that the equation is more complex. However, it is possible – or, more accurately, it is possible with a glassfibre boat and at the time of construction. Foam is injected between inner and outer hull skin, under berths, and often in the bilge space. Foam or balsa core construction also add some positive buoyancy. Integral foam entails a sacrifice of stowage space, but this is a small price to pay for peace of mind. However, it is difficult (if not impossible) to fill and bond foam to cavities once the hull has been built and, for constructional reasons, not advisable to do so in a timber boat (certainly not with one of 'traditional type'). Later on, if there is any injury to the external hull, the presence of the foam will make repairs both difficult and expensive. Air bags are another alternative; how-ever, they must be carefully sited and attached to strong points so that they cannot break loose and (literally) tear apart the hull and deck of a waterlogged boat.

As for capsizing – well, it is a fact that there are circum-stances under which any boat can be knocked down (a knock-

Fig 15 (Opposite) **Static stability curves:** Narrow boats heel faster, but also have the larger stability-reserve (safe zone). The righting lever is applied above the heeling angle. The so-called 'negative sta-bility' for the larger boat (with the higher centre of gravity) is already at just over 90 degrees. If this angle is exceeded, the boat will not right itself on its own accord.

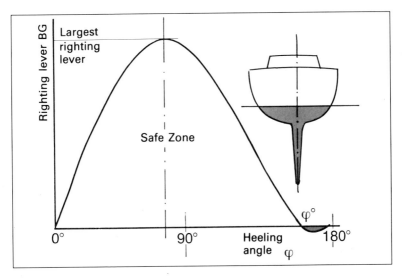

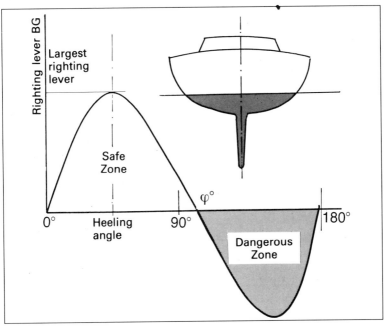

down is where the boat is flat on its side, with the hull at 90 degrees to the surface of the water). Indeed, this is not even an uncommon occurrence, particularly where racing boats are concerned. Far more serious is complete inversion, though this is usually the result of freak conditions and is fortunately far less common. Although, as has already been said, it is impossible to give an absolute guarantee that such disasters will *never* occur, they are very unlikely in a well-designed cruising boat with good lateral stability and a high reserve of buoyancy inherent in topsides and superstructure. A keel boat, whose hull measurements are within normal parameters, will (so long as the ballast calculations are correct) always right itself from a knock-down and even after a complete inversion (but in either case this is dependent upon a watertight hull with hatches and flushing boards remaining in place). The speed with which the boat returns upright depends on the position of the centre of gravity G and the centre of buoyancy B for every heeling angle. This is the basis of the so-called 'still water stability', displayed as a curve. Applied above the heeling angle, it displays the height of uprighting moments.

When the curve cuts through the line of the heeling angle it is divided into two zones, the one above the heeling angle is the safe zone and the other one the dangerous zone. The intersection is known as the 'negative stability' (point of capsizing). It is easy to establish a yacht's stability by using this curve, but unfortunately you will not be able to obtain it as a buyer; you have to rely on the designer. Generally speaking, it can be said that boats with long keels and a low centre of gravity (which can roughly be estimated from the proportion of ballast) are far less prone to capsizing than modern designs with flat underwater hulls and fin keels. Cut-away keels and long-keelers are also generally capable of righting themselves if they turn turtle. This is precisely what wide-beamed boats with a shallow bottom do not do; they remain upside down for minutes and only the impetus of a wave or something similar will turn the boat back vertically. A structure of large volume that supplies buoyancy after the capsize would change this. Unfortunately, many cruiser/racers have flush decks (thanks to their origination from racing yachts) that make things worse.

So much for the static stability that is important in still water – unfortunately, the dynamic stability is harder to detect. Consequently, little is known about it. One thing, though, seems definite; the larger the yacht, the more force is needed by the breaking sea in order to capsize it. In order to capsize a 9-metre boat, you would in theory need a 6-metre-high wave. Light yachts are especially susceptible to capsizing as they accelerate faster. A high freeboard, which is an advantage for the static stability, offers a larger attacking area for the waves. What about the fin keel? Dynamically, it has the advantage of stalling less in breaking seas than a long keel does (as described in many experience reports), but once the yacht has been knocked down, the static stability takes over and thereby it is important for a yacht to return to its normal sailing position. These aspects should also be criteria for consideration when you are deciding which boat to buy. A light fin-keeler, in spite of its size, should only be recommended for sailing along safe coasts in the hands of experienced sailors.

5 Construction features: viewing yachts at boat shows

The design features of a boat will allow you to assess whether it has been built for speed, rough seas, light winds or only for day sailing. With the information given in the following chapters, you should be able to determine a boat's character, ie whether it is course stable, cuts smoothly into seas, or whether it requires stronger winds in order to reach the hull speed.

Lateral plan

The first thing to catch your eye when looking at a docked yacht is the lateral plan. This is the term for the lateral area of the underwater hull. It is part of the yacht's overall picture, and although you can probably see the length of the boat above water from the profile, the lateral plan will provide better information regarding the yacht's characteristics. After all, it has to produce the lateral force in the water to counterbalance the force of the sail and simultaneously provide course stability. Here, the flattened surface area is the first priority.

Boats with flat lines and fin keels make things slightly more difficult, because the lateral profile and the keel profile offer sufficient buoyancy. They can be compared to the main features of a hdyrofoil, even if the keel hangs vertically in the water. It follows (see 'Manoeuvrability and course stability', p. 28) that the longer and narrower a wing, the more buoyancy it produces and the narrower (theoretically) can be its profile.

The best option for a cruising yacht is a compromise between the width of the keel and acceptable draught. A wide keel (approaching long keel) also has a better keel-to-hull transition. The distance from the keel to the rudder is also of interest; the rudder is more effective the longer the lever is between

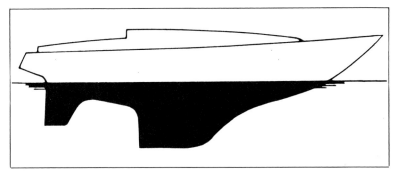

Fig 16 The lateral plan: This displays the complete underwater profile, which is responsible for minimising drifting angles; thus good
height to windward. These cut-away keelers have proved themselves as pleasant cruising yachts.

the keel's and rudder's centre of effort. Another important consideration is whether the designer provides a skeg or whether
the rudder hangs freely. A skeg produces a free water flow
around the rudder and provides additional lateral area for a
better course stability. The lateral plan also displays whether
a boat reacts sluggishly or sensitively to rudder movement and
whether it needs drive to stop the boat from drifting. A narrow
fin always needs speed for developing buoyancy. A large lateral plan also has higher friction resistance because of her large
wetted surface. The proportion of the rudder's area should be
5–7 per cent of the lateral plan for a long-keeler and 10–12 per
cent for short-keeled boats. Yachts with these values have
proved to be easy to steer.

Midship section

A complete drawing plan that provides a two-dimensional view
of all sections offers you the best idea of a boat's hull shape.
These drawings are seldom available, so you will have to be sat-
isfied with the midship section. The midship section is where
the boat's widest beam is. It describes the largest circumference
and cross-section. If you are unable to obtain a drawing, you

can instead view a boat from the front and back at a boat show or in boatyards (take a photo!). It will allow you to find out more about the boat's character. A car's equivalent to the midship section is its so-called 'frontal area', which is used for determining the C_W-value. The midship section is also of importance for the resistance. As the cross-section of the yacht's submerged area, the resistance is a criterion for the cylinder coefficient that was mentioned in 'Fast sailing' (p. 23; and described in the Appendix). At first glance, the section gives information on storage space, living area and headroom and also clarifies the bilge section. The shape of the midship section permits assumptions regarding form stability; flat, bowl-shaped ones possess a larger righting moment than semi-circular ones.

The shape of the keel displays the lateral force and the circumference of the midship section will tell you whether the wetted surface of the boat will be large or small. For a fine-weather boat you should choose the narrow hull shape of a

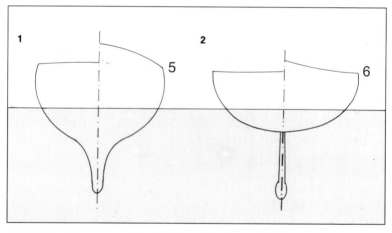

Fig 17 Section-curves 5 and 6 describe the midship section. It is defined as the section of the largest beam and determines the boat's degree of volume (cylinder coefficient). The midship section and the length determine a yacht's shape. Diagram **1** is a heavy displacement yacht, as you can see from its S-shaped transition from keel to the hull, while diagram **2** shows a light displacement yacht with fin keel.

heavy displacement yacht, and for a heavy-weather boat, the wider hull shape.

Chine sections

Again and again you will come across boats with hard chine sections, although this building method is not necessary for GRP yachts. It is a simple and cheap method of construction used for boats made of plywood (such as the Buccaneer or Naja) or steel, as the material is simply planked without compound curves. Sharp corners are more difficult to produce in GRP yachts. Some designers still seem convinced of the superiority of their GRP hard chine construction, although surveys have proved them wrong – at least with cruising yachts, which generally don't exceed their hull speed. At low speeds, round-bilged hulls definitely display lower resistance in the water and are therefore faster.

Only in planing conditions – mainly motor boats with sufficient speed – does the hard chine construction show an advantage. When a hard chine hull displaces water, it produces a premature detachment of the streamflow, which is the reason for the higher resistance. This makes the hard chine shape only sensible for ultra-light constructions that are sailed to plane or for self-builders who are able by this means to obtain a larger yacht.

Keels

Nowadays, long-keeled yachts are often regarded as heavy motorsailers. With lighter yachts, the choice lies between keels with small aspect ratios or fin keels with large profiles. A cruising yacht's keel should be closer to a long keel, so that the boat is able to use shallow harbours and is also in a position to lie safely in drying harbours. The area of such a keel should be about 4 per cent of the sail area.

Keels are often mounted so that they slope aft. If this has no

How to choose the right yacht

practical reason, ie attachment to the hull or shifting the ballast further aft, there is no reason to do this – though one exception might be in boats with a large fin area relative to draught, as these can achieve greater effectiveness by sloping the keel aft.

The keel's profile is important for a good lateral force; the curve of the front edge, the largest thickness of the profile in relation to length and the position of the greatest thickness all have a profound effect on efficiency. NACA profiles (as already mentioned) are generally used, which are assembled and already calculated in the book *Theory of Wing Sections*. In designer circles, these profiles are known as the measure of all profiles. NACA profiles have an elliptic inlet (front edge) and an acute outrunning end. They are a sign of good buoyancy to windward and are evidence of the fact that the designer has given some thought to the hydrodynamics of his boat.

A keel's circumference is also of importance with regard to a boat's lateral force underway: if you disregard long narrow fins as only suitable for racing yachts, you will find that rectangular keels offer slightly more buoyancy than trapezoid-shaped ones. Keels with an elliptic circumference are slightly more favourable. For practical reasons you should choose a long bottom edge that runs parallel to the waterline (for a cruiser), so that the boat can easily be placed on its winter hard standing.

(Opposite) Because boatyards mostly withhold the drawing plan from the customer, it is important for the buyer to actually look at the midship section. Here, you will see whether the boat has a U-, V- or semi-circular hull shape. You can estimate from the acuteness of the bow and the flat bottom how the boat cuts into waves. Flat-bottomed hulls cut in harder than, for example, the S-section of a long-keeler. Having said that, a thin fin keel with a hard chine to a flat-bottomed hull promises good lateral buoyancy. The hydrodynamic bulb keel shown in photo **2** on p.52 (Scheel-keel, named after the American designer Scheel) offers optimal lateral force with a low draught.

Fig 18 Most modern yachts are fin-keeled, though these are available in many types – which suggests that there is no ideal keel! The keels shown in the diagram are hydrofoils with large buoyancy, but offer lower course stability (this is produced by the alignment of the keel and the rudder). They are suitable as a keel – and also as a rudder-form. Diagram **1** displays the most important measurements of a mounted keel. A and B in diagram **2** show straight fins, and C and D show angled fins. The keel shape is dependent upon the mounting option to the hull. The width and depth of the keel is important for performance to windward, depending on

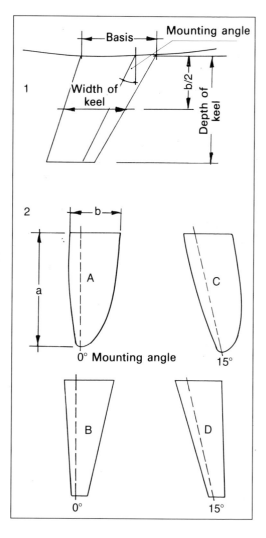

the relationship between profile a and b. The mounting angle has little influence on the yacht's sailing performance.

Winged keels

Some cruising yachts have adapted the winged keel (keel with side-wings) after it appeared on the successful 12 metre yacht *Australia II*. The argument was that it would give more height to windward with less draught by concentrating the ballast in the wings. This has proved to be untrue. The flow around the keel (like a hydrofoil) might be bettered (like the endplate, which prevents the flow from drifting away), but this advantage turns into a disadvantage in heavier seas when the boat is pitching.

The draught can only be reduced if the proportion of ballast is increased, because the righting lever becomes smaller. This would be more effective with a 'bulb' at the bottom end of the keel. If the bulb keel is also designed as a hydrodynamic shape like the Scheel-keel, it will be even better. The special lines of this keel, as used by many designers, have originated in a test tank and look rather iron-shaped.

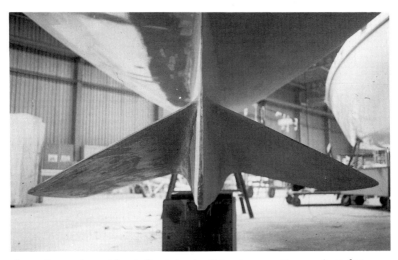

A modern winged keel: Such keels did not prove themselves for cruising yachts as they reduce the boat's speed ahead when it is pitching. They do, however, carry the ballast further down, so that the boat's draught can be reduced.

Rudders

If a sailing boat is left to its own devices it becomes unstable around its vertical axis with regard to headway. Course stability is produced by the rudder, which reduces the yawing and steers the boat. Rudders of older-style cruising yachts are placed at the aft edge of the conventional long keel, which makes these yachts difficult to turn but extremely reliable in heavy seas. With the appearance of the divided lateral plans, as in the fin keels, the rudder was elongated and moved further and further below the stern to give stability.

Counterbalancing the rudder's centre of effort with that of the keel and the sail area is an art that is not possessed by every designer. The rudder should have an optimal effect in every heeling angle, but this is often not achieved. For balance reasons, the geometrical lateral centre of effort should be behind the sail's geometrical centre of effort; applied to the waterline, the distance required between both centres is between 10 and 15 per cent.

Rudders can be built like keels, preferably with a large aspect ratio: long and narrow. The NACA-profile offers a very good rudder movement, but is very sensitive and is not forgiving of mistakes. If the angle of the rudder is too large, the stream of water cuts off and the boat shoots off course.

Smaller ratios of rudder profiles are less critical. A good investment for cruising yachts is also a skeg, as free-hanging spade rudders are more suitable for racing yachts, and most sailors will not require that much sensitivity.

Designers like a balanced rudder blade so that the rotating axis does not affect the front edge of the rudder; and any effects will be experienced somewhere aft. The rudder area is therefore divided into a front area and a balanced area. Depending on whether the rudder's centre of effort lies in front or aft of the rotation axis defines the terms under- or over-balanced rudder. A balanced rudder puts less pressure on the tiller because the front area supports the required force. The ideal rudder should have its centre of effort slightly behind the rotating axis, so that the helmsman still feels a little pressure on the rudder.

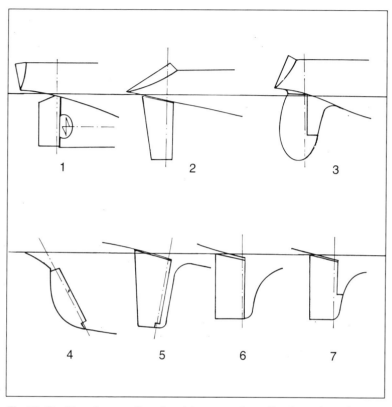

Fig 19 Rudder shapes: Good rudders are also effective when the boat is heeled, for example the long keel rudder shown in **1** and **4**. Spade rudders (**2**) tend to cavitate, ie suck air and lose their effect. They can be too sensitive for cruising yachts. The rudder shown in diagram **3** often has problems with seaweed, which gets stuck between the fin and the rudder, as is also the case in diagram **7**. The rudders in diagrams **5** and **6** have proved themselves as sensible for cruising yachts: they are placed safely behind a skeg and are forgiving of small steering mistakes.

57

Cruising yachts should sail with a slight weatherhelm, which is also optimal for the rudder. The rudder has to be set at a slight angle, so that the stream from the keel catches the rudder at a favourable angle. Rudders of modern yachts are generally positioned directly under the stern in order to achieve the best steering. You can check out whether your dream boat is designed in this way.

Part of the rudder is lifted out of the water if the stern is lifted by waves coming from behind, or if boats with a beamy quarter are sailing with a large heeling angle. You should pay attention to this when buying a boat. A partial solution to this effect would be a deep rudder with skeg. Spade rudders in particular lose their efficiency when heeling at large angles because a cavitation effect causes the rudder to suck air and renders it totally useless.

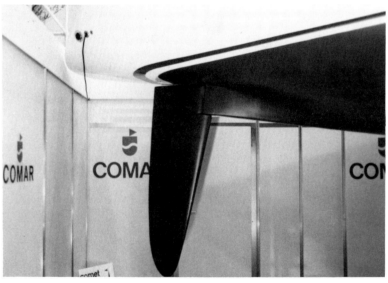

1

Balanced rudders, even with partial skegs, are not totally problem free. Seaweed, ropes or plastic bags can easily become trapped between skeg and rudder blade and impair the function (**1** and **2**).

2

3

This cannot happen with front-balanced rudders (**3**). All these rudders also have skegs that, as you can see, can be completely different in design.

Skeg and distance to the centre of gravity

The rudder area is a part of the lateral area, so it makes sense to design it large in order to increase the lateral plan for a reduction of the leeway. The disadvantage is that it places larger forces on the rudder. The skeg in front of the rudder is therefore a good solution in various respects: the actual rudder area is placed safely behind the fin and is easier to mount. The boat is also easier on the rudder, ie it is not too lively, and does not oversteer easily.

The skeg serves as a good leading edge for the rudder. The rudder can also be partially balanced behind this area. A cruising sailor's most important argument for a rudder with a

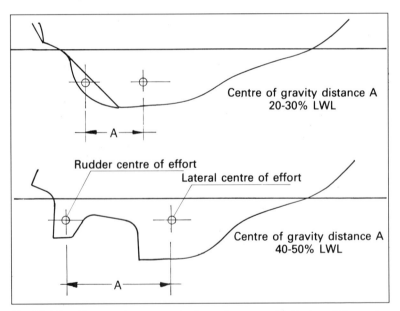

Fig 20 The distance between the lateral centre of effort and the rudder's centre of effort is an important criterion in addition to the rudder's hydrodynamic qualities. The short keel comes out better. However, such rudders easily emerge far aft at the hull and are less protected. A skeg in front of the rudder is therefore very important.

skeg is that mooring lines, plastic bags and weed or barnacles can cause little damage. Such things are always a threat to free-standing rudders.

The distance between the lateral areas of keel and rudder are vital to the effectiveness of the rudder. Momentum develops when moving the rudder (force times righting lever); thus, the shorter the distance between the centres of effort, the smaller is the effectiveness of the rudder. If a long-keeler is compared to a fin-keeler, it becomes obvious (apart from the fact that there is water flow between rudder and keel) that a long-keeled boat manoeuvres more sluggishly. Its rudder momentum calculates levers with values between 20 and 35 per cent of the length of the waterline, while short-keelers achieve levers between 40 and 50 per cent LWL.

Bow shapes

The bow shape gives the yacht its characteristic appearance and is responsible for the way it cuts through the water and whether it sails dry or wet. This has little to do with the angle of the bow (seen from its side), ie whether it is extremely angled or straight, with hollow lines (clipper bow), or convex (spoon bow). A straight bow only increases the flotation line.

Bows with a classic deep forefoot (usually in connection with a pointed V-shaped bow) contribute to good sea behaviour. Extreme fin-keelers generally have a shallow forefoot. On modern yachts you generally find a shallow forefoot which turns into a trapezoid-shaped hull. You can already recognise this on the flat bottom in the forward area. In squalls, this prevents the increased weather helm that is common with flat-bottomed boats. In slight seas these bows sail without a large bow wave, and if the boat is light enough – rarely the case with cruising yachts – it planes more easily. In heavier seas it pounds more quickly, unless sailing with a sufficiently large heeling angle. In such cases, the edge of the trapezoid section enters the water first and not the flat bottom. The fullness of the bow and the angle it cuts into the water – or, if you prefer, the sharpness of the bow – becomes important. A sharp bow that runs into a pointed forefoot has less resistance in the water than a fuller one. However, a boat like this can carry less sail as it has less buoyancy. If it could carry a large genoa, it would probably undercut. For these boats, designers have allowed for a smaller genoa or constructed the boat with a fractional (7/8)-rig.

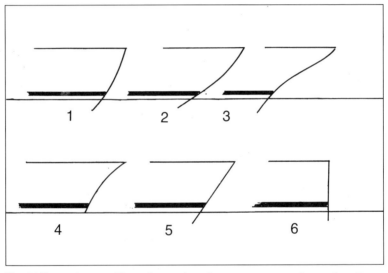

Fig 21 Bow shapes: They determine the appearance of a yacht; diagram **6** has the longest LWL, while the bow in diagram **3** has the shortest. All other shapes are in between. Some shapes have got specific names like clipper bow (**3**) or spoon bow (**2**). Modern yachts are generally built with straight, raked bows (**5**).

In order to cut smoothly into the sea, the bow and the shape of the forefoot should be designed to produce more buoyancy when further dipping into the sea, ie smoothly cutting into the water without abrupt braking effects. The angle at which the boat cuts into the water is also known as the angle between the waterline and the longitudinal axis of the boat (seen from above). It is dependent on the breadth and the position of the midship section and determines the bow shape.

The admission angle (point of entry into the water) of small boats (ie less than 8 metres) is determined from the required width of the bottom end of the forepeak berths. As they generally come together with the waterline, you can measure the admission angle at this location: it should not exceed more than 26 degrees for a seakindly yacht (see page 66).

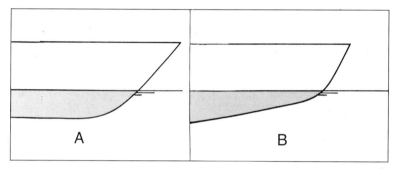

Fig 22 The shape of the fore gripe (forefoot) gives a clue about the boat's speed and height to windward: Diagram **A** is good for oncoming seas. Boats with such a distinctive forefoot are able to point high. Diagram **B**: Less forefoot suggests a flat bottom and therefore fast hull.

The shape of the forefoot determines the trim of the yacht when heeled. If it is too narrow, the stern lifts when the boat heels, which slows down the speed and the bow will probably undercut. In addition, you would have a lot of pressure on the rudder and bad manoeuvrability. If the forefoot is too bulky, the stern will be pressed on to the water and the bow lifts. This also reduces the speed, the boat goes off-course, and the action of the rudder exacerbates this further. The relation between bow and stern should therefore be balanced. The position of the midship section (on the middle of the waterline length) serves as a good indicator.

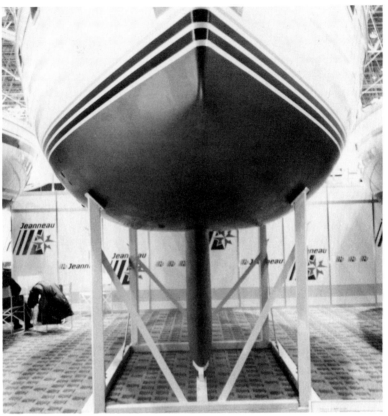

1

The flat bottom (photo **1**) has a larger area in the water than the beamy V (photo **2**). The fact that it cuts in smoother is an additional factor. A flat bottom is only worthwhile for light designs that start planing quickly. A flat bottom is inappropriate for heavy boats that do not exceed their hull speed.

2

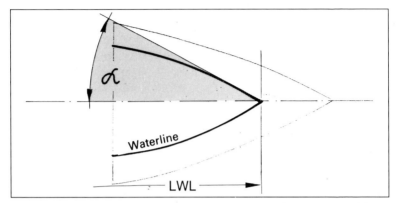

Fig 23 The entry angle determines whether a yacht cuts smoothly or hard into the water. It is the angle between the boat's longitudinal axis and the tangent of the bow's waterline, and depends on the relation V/√LWL (see table below). A high displacement, depending on the LWL, produces small entry angles and therefore smooth cutting into seas.

V/√LWL	α (IE)
0.5	30°
0.6	26°
0.7	22°
0.8	18°
0.9	14°
1.0...2.0	10°

Stern

The stern influences the yacht's performance even more than the bow. While a wide bow may enhance speed at some points, a badly constructed stern which has no clean stream flow is useless. The boat gets out of trim and drags through excess water turbulence. One old boatbuilder's rule says, 'A boat must lose water at the stern' and this still applies. The stern should therefore be designed accordingly: if a natural water flow follows its natural lines, it will flow smoothly and without interruption. It can then stream off the stern without turbulence – and it is turbulence that creates unnecessary resistance. The wave resistance that stops a boat's drive increases the higher the stern wave develops. You recognise this on the steep slope of the run aft. It leads the water unnecessarily high without letting the flow cut off. A boat with a flat hull shape and correspondingly flat stern sails faster than a boat that lies deeper in the water and has a worse water flow.

The height of the stern wave provides a good indicator of performance. While a pointed stern is sufficient for a rowing boat (normally the most favourable hydrodynamic form to lose the water), a yacht's stern needs to be wide (because of the higher speed) with more displacement so that it does not drop into the wave trough that develops at the stern. The faster a boat, the longer is the wave it sails on.

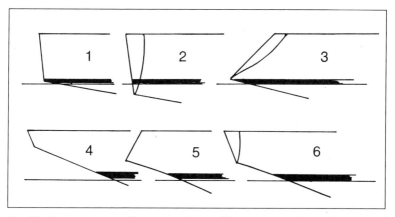

Fig 24 Stern shapes: The stern shape, like the bow shape (ie overhangs), can increase the length of the waterline when the boat is heeled and this increases a yacht's speed (**4, 5** and **6**). Nowadays, the stern is generally designed so that it always produces a maximum LWL (**1, 2** and **3**).

Flat sterns arise naturally, following through from the flat midship section in light displacement yachts. A light weight only displaces a small amount of water, so that less volume is submerged: this allows the hull shape to be flat. If more weight, ie displacement, is added (as is generally the case with cruisers), the midship section needs to become deeper; this automatically results in steeper sterns that are then only useful for displacement boats. If you want to exceed this, the boat has to become lighter. The IOR-racing rules punish flat sterns (so that the advantage of extreme designs is not as great). This is why some designers built sterns that sloped unnecessarily steeply and, in essence, designed poor boats.

Even displacement yachts should not have a declining angle (indicates the steepness of the stern) of more than 20 degrees. A yacht with a larger displacement astern has a longer breadth waterline, which produces more resistance at low speeds and lifts the rudder out of the water when the boat is heeled. Excessive hollow stern shapes indicate that the boat 'sucks water' when the speed increases. Flat stretched stern shapes indicate speeds exceeding the hull speed, so long as the stern is not overloaded with holiday gear – and the crew trims the displacement centre!

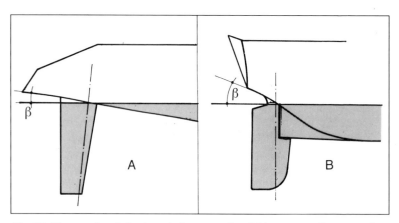

Fig 25 The angle of the boat's bottom should be as small as possible (β<10 degrees), which can only be realised in light displacement yachts (**A**). Heavy cruisers have an angle of up to 35 degrees (**B**). Small angles encourage the water flow and increase the boat's speed, while large angles produce resistance.

Rigging

A yacht's rig produces the forward drive: to windward through air flow on the sails' profile; before the wind by building up pressure in as much canvas as possible. You can already detect from the rig whether the vessel is a stable cruiser or a fast racing boat; while the first is built more solidly, fast boats generally have slimmer mast profiles and as little rigging as possible. The rigging is attached so as to form the lowest resistance possible for the wind.

A 'fast' rig can also be suitable for a cruising yacht, so long as it is both strong and simple, although in strong winds the length of the hull's waterline in any case limits the boat's speed (rarely more than $2.43\sqrt{LWL}$). In lighter winds with speeds below the hull speed, a high-performance rig can extract more from the wind by allowing an optimal mast tune for a better trim of the mainsail.

The wire rigging of many cruising yachts could be improved by orientating itself to racing boats, because the rig with most stays is not necessarily the most solid or even the most effective: the sail drive should be designed for courses close to the wind. Therefore, it is important to have a well-fixed rig without unnecessary air resistance, and a stiff boat that offers the wind a large sail area without much heeling. All other courses will then follow naturally.

The most effective rig is one with the largest stretch of sail, which means the higher and narrower (at equal area) it is, the faster it sails. Cruising yachts, regardless of whether they are fast or slow, should be easy to handle as they are mostly sailed by families. They therefore require a simple user-friendly rig, which is still easily adaptable to the wind conditions. The less complicated the construction, the better. The masthead should be kept simple; this applies to the halyards, but also to the stays.

Masthead rigs

Most cruisers are masthead-rigged sloops (single-masted sailing boats), as was the case with RORC racing yachts during the 1960s. Because this type of rig can be very solid, at times having several crosstrees, it has proved itself right up to the present time and is still in use. Cruising yachts should not adopt the extra-large foresails and the narrow main, as these represent the 1960s racing formulas and require continuous sail changes. The disadvantage of the masthead rig is unwieldy foresails with large winches, as well as little opportunity for trimming. The advantage is the simplicity without running backstays.

Fractional rigs

This type of rigging is currently in favour, although it is not new. It is more flexible than the masthead rig. Because the forestay is attached to the mast at about 7/8 of its height (the measure is not fixed – it could also be at 3/4 or 5/6 of the mast height), it allows the masthead to flex in gusts. This slackens the leach and stretches it automatically when the gust is over, just as it should do. If the mast is slightly flexible, the mainsail will flatten automatically in stronger winds. However, the fractional rig requires running backstays that have to be set accurately, and these might stretch the capabilities of a family crew when tacking or gybing in heavy-sea conditions. The advantage is a handier foresail, which is usually quite small. (You will also not require two different-sized foresails, as the fractional rig gets its main drive from the (large) mainsail, which is also easy to handle.)

Angled crosstrees

A gentler version of the fractional rig is a mast with 25 to 30 degrees aft-angled spreaders. The angled shrouds are acting towards the forestay, which makes having a standing backstay unnecessary. This solution is not as effective as backstays, since the forestay normally sags when sailing to windward. The shrouds must therefore be extremely tight, which is only possible for a boat of up to about 10 metres. Another disadvan-

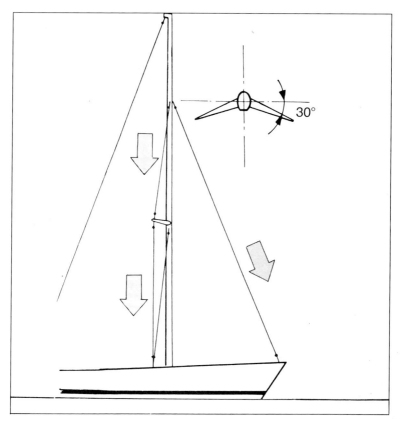

Fig 26 The characteristic fractional rig with its forestay attached about 1/4 below the masthead. It is more complicated than the masthead rig because of the backstays. Therefore, cruising boats are often fitted with angled spreaders, which allows the mast rigging to be without a standing backstay. The pull of the forestay is absorbed from the upper spreader. Fractional rigged masts allow an optimal mast trim because they are flexible. The angle of the crosstrees is often less than 30 degrees.

tage is that the mainsail chafes on the spreaders and shrouds if it is let out when sailing downwind. The non-existent backstay might compensate for this.

Cutter-rigs

The cutter-rig has been slightly out of favour, but it is now coming back into fashion and offers cruising yachts an ideal option by dividing the foretriangle area into a jib and staysail (instead of a genoa). An inner and outer forestay are required, and sometimes also running backstays in order to compensate for the pull of the inner forestay.

Two-masters

Of the typical two-masted boats (schooner, ketch and yawl), only the ketch is still mass-produced. From an aerodynamic view, the mizzen mast is not worth the money. When sailed to windward it only produces resistance, and before the wind the mizzen sail blankets the main. The only time it might be useful is when sailing on a beam reach – and for carrying the radar scanner that is difficult to attach on to a sloop.

Mast profiles

An effective rig should produce as little wind resistance as possible. This applies to excessive wires, such as additional shrouds, and diagonal rigging (which is not always necessary) – and, of course, the mast profile itself. A mast that is especially thick does not necessarily mean that it is also very solid: its resistance momentum opposes the bending that is derived from the momentum of inertia.

The momentum of inertia is produced from the area of the cross-section multiplied by the square of its distance from a neutral axis (see Fig 28). A thick profile wall with little distance from the mast centre line can be as solid as a small wall with larger distance. Only wind resistance and weight are different; therefore, the speed-orientated buyer will purchase the profile with the more favourable resistance.

One trick when handling thin masts is to sail them with a slight bend. With a tightened standing backstay, the mast will pump less in stronger winds and the material will not fatigue as quickly. This is also acceptable to a sceptical buyer who

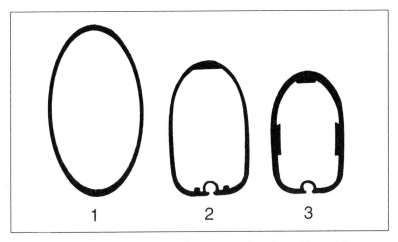

Fig 27 In comparison to the earlier conventional oval form (**1**), mast sections are nowadays built in box form (**2** and **3**). They are easy to bend for mast rake aft. The sail track is already built in to the profile.

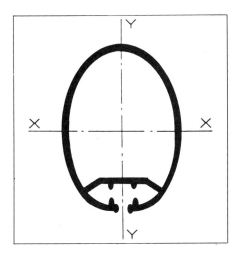

Fig 28 The resistance momentum of the mast's section is responsible for the mast's stability. It depends on the wall of the theoretical axis X and Y. Thin profiles with thick walls have bend equivalent to thick sections with thin walls. Big masts are easy to build, but the fragile-looking masts of racing yachts are not quite as fragile as they look; therefore they are not as light.

wants a solid mast. Another factor is that the sail becomes flatter, which should anyway be the aim in stronger winds; one is automatically presented with the right trim. Nevertheless, such things assist in alleviating the fear of racing rigs of many a sailor. An effective rig is not simply the one with the highest mast, but also the one with least wind resistance. Even in a force 4 it should produce sufficient energy to bring a boat up to its hull speed without excessive heeling.

Engines

The yacht's engine must be carefully considered because it can adversely affect performance under sail: a designer who knows his job will therefore ensure that this machinery is no larger or heavier than necessary to provide auxiliary power, and will attempt to keep it sited as low in the hull as possible – perhaps even integrating it into the righting ballast. (By this token, the best site would be at the bottom of the keel, but, as this is clearly impracticable, as close to its upper surface as possible is the most appropriate location – at least here it is close to the centre of gravity and not adding undesirable weight to the ends of the boat.) In this position, however, the engine will obtrude into the saloon and not everyone is prepared to sacrifice living space or, for that matter, to tolerate engine noise. (Here, it would at least be accessible for maintenance or major overhaul, although this is not invariably so: there are cases where yachts appear to have been moulded around the engine and this makes repairs virtually impossible without dismantling joinery, and perhaps even cutting through internal mouldings.)

Largely because of the weight factor, no sailing boat should have installed an engine that is larger than necessary; no horsepower on earth will ever propel it at more than the designed hull speed! An overlarge engine may even prevent this speed being reached, since the extra avoirdupois will cause the stern to squat and thus induce greater resistance. This is in fact a good example of the law of diminishing returns!

It is difficult to generalise about engine power, as so much depends upon the weight, shape and waterline length of the hull, and also the amount of motoring envisaged: is the engine only to be used to stem a foul tide in light airs? Or will it be relied upon to thrust the boat home through heavy weather? The best advice is always obtained from the engine manufacturer or main agent, who will also specify such matters as the maximum angle of installation (and the maximum angle of heel at which the motor may safely be run: this last a very important consideration, particularly for any yacht that makes a habit of motorsailing).

Propellers

The propeller and stern gear (be that a shaft and bracket or a saildrive unit) also have a direct bearing upon sailing performance – after all, every appendage below the waterline is a source of drag! Fin-keelers are more suited to a saildrive with folding propeller than a fixed shaft with fixed propeller, so long as the prop is situated in front of the rudder so that prop thrust streams past the rudder. It is less speed reducing because of the favourable flow around the shaft. The shaft can be designed in different ways. The form with the smallest resistance is still the folding propeller without shaft bracket. Its resistance values are below those of the saildrive. Another acceptable solution is a shaft coming out from some sort of skeg. Behind it, a two-bladed prop can be rested in 'sail position', which is probably the best compromise in order to satisfy the boat's motoring and sailing performance. You should keep clear of shaft installations that do not possess hydrodynamically formed shaft brackets and fixed props. These systems can cause speed loss of up to a knot (see also p. 101).

Another piece of hydrodynamic nonsense is to run the prop in an aperture that is cut in the rudder blade. Fortunately, this solution is rarely seen these days, for the section of the rudder blade only invokes additional resistance in the form of turbulence, whereby the rudder is not subject to the optimal thrust stream of the prop. The largest part of the water stream shoots through the screw aperture, so manoeuvring under engine is difficult.

Profiled shaft brackets and saildrive shafts also add additional lateral area to the boat, although the best engine for a small boat (below 2 ton displacement) is still arguably the outboard, which can be stowed in a locker with its only contribution towards sailing being its weight. It is only good, though, if the boat sails; any inboard engine is better for motoring. The disadvantages of outboards are their tendency to emerge from the water when the boat is pitching, bad distribution of ballast (even when installed in a trunking) and poor efficiency of a small, too highly rotating prop that cannot be adapted properly (construction reasons: cavitation plate) to a displacement yacht.

6 Making comparisons of ratios at home

Ever since yachts were first built, people have been trying to find criteria for evaluating them. Length and width are fixed, but displacement and sail area can easily be adjusted. Whether a yacht really offers a pleasant sail and whether it actually reaches hull speed in a force 3 (according to the dealer), although it is under-rigged, cannot be established at a glance. You just have to take the dealer's word for it! Only coefficients from the boat's main measurements can help you to evaluate a boat. The ratios allow comparisons with other boats and characterise the yacht's qualities. The results are extremely close to measured values.

The waterline length (LWL), breadth on the waterline (BWL), displacement (V) and sail area (AS) are considered in relation to one another, as boatbuilders and designers would also do when evaluating a yacht. While professionals still use the calculator in order to obtain coefficients, all you have to do in this book is to study the diagrams: two measurements from the brochure will give you more details about the boat's qualities. For example, in order to calculate the waterline-displacement coefficient, you read the waterline length of the horizontal axis in Fig 31 with the displacement of the vertical axis. This tells you where your yacht is positioned: is it a heavy or light displacement boat? Or is it somewhere in between?

Each of the introduced numbers states whether a boat is relatively narrow- or wide-beamed, over- or under-rigged, fast or slow, heavy or light. Sailing performance and sailing characteristics depend on these values, but it is difficult to view them simultaneously. Diagrams are a perfect method of determining the coefficients and offer a clear overview. The arrows indicate in which direction a boat's tendencies lie. If you use the provided diagrams with all the boats of your choice, the decision as to which is the most suitable will be quite easy. In order to work out dimensionless values, the sail area takes its value from the second root $\sqrt{AS}$ and the displacement gets the value from the third root $^3\sqrt{V}$. Therefore, you will be able to compare the displacement in m^3 and the sail area in m^2 and the length and width (metres) in direct relation to the other values.

Length–beam ratio

Is the boat too beamy or too narrow? This question cannot be answered with a yardstick. You can only find out whether a boat is narrow or wide, and the resulting effects, if you put it into the context of length. The breadth of the waterline is an indicator of a boat's behaviour at sea and her tacking qualities. When applied to the length of the waterline, it produces a number of lines that represent wide boats if they go to the top left and narrow designs if they go to the bottom right-hand corner of the diagram. Coefficients for normal beamed boats are between the values of 2.8 and 3.2. The advantages for boat 1 in Fig 29 are clear; because of its breadth, the boat is good on a close reach, but will tack badly with extensive heeling. Boat 2 will be good close to windward, but will have to reef early.

Sail area–waterline ratio

Is a yacht tender or stiff? The waterline area applied above the sail area will give this information. Again, you can detect tendencies. Because the BWL is responsible for the form, or initial stability, the lines in Fig 30 in connection with the sail area indicate some sort of sail-carrying ability that is, strictly speaking, only for boats with a high proportion of form stability, especially for centreboarders or keel centreboarders. If a keel boat is heeled, the proportion of the weight stability is added, so that it is better to put displacement in relation to the sail area. The lines differentiate in each case between a stiff and a tender boat and therefore indicate whether it behaves

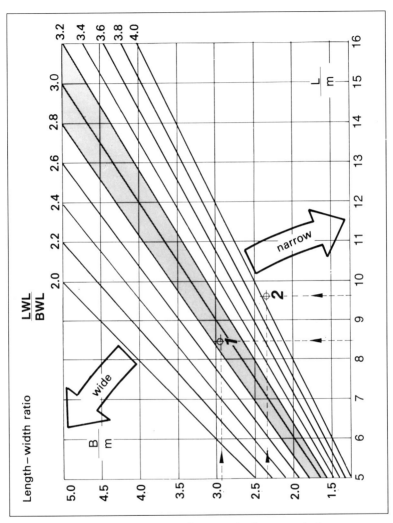

Fig 29 The length–width ratio tells you whether a yacht is narrow-or wide-beamed. A modern yacht is considered normal if her values are between 2.8 and 3.2. A boat is narrow if her values are above this and wide if they are below. For determining the coefficient, you apply the boat's breadth from the vertical axis to the right and her length from the horizontal axis to the top. The intersection displays where the boat lies in relation to the others.

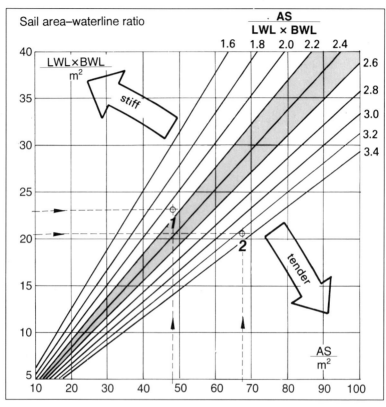

Fig 30 The sail area in relation to the waterline rectangle (from LWL times BWL) indicates whether a yacht is stiff or tender. If its values lie between 2.2 and 2.6, it will react with normal heeling angles in gusts; if the values lie above 2.6 it will heel steeply. Values below 2.2 indicate a stiff boat. Apply the sum of LWL and BWL, starting from the vertical axis to the right and the sail area (main and no 1 genoa) from the horizontal axis to the top. The intersection tells you where your boat is in relation to others.

pleasantly or awkwardly in heavier seas. Too much initial stability (boat 1 in Fig 30) prevents smooth sailing in gusts. A yacht that snaps upright abruptly is not very pleasant for crew and gear. The lines in the diagram also indicate how many square metres of canvas a boat has per square metre of floating water area, ie whether it is over- or under-canvased. This is handy for comparing boats quickly (except for extreme types). Boats with values between 2.2 and 2.6 are well mannered at sea.

Length–displacement ratio

Is the boat light or heavy? If you apply the boat's displacement to the length, it will give you a clue as to whether it is light or heavy and whether it is fast or slow with equal sail area. In some literature you find the term $V(LWL/10)^3$. A diagram allows differentiations between heavy displacement yachts, normal displacement, light displacement and ultralight displacement boats. This length–displacement ratio is a measure of how much boat-weight is distributed across the given waterline. A heavy displacement boat is therefore a boat with a large displacement in the water.

For our method, the ratio is more suitable the other way around, ie $LWL/3\sqrt{V}$ (Fig 31). The coefficients of a heavy displacement yacht lie between 4.0 and 5.0; light displacement yachts are between 6.0 and 8.0. In strong winds, boat 1 in Fig 31 sails faster than heavier designs because of the low displacement and flat hull shape, while in light winds boat 2 will be faster. Boats with narrower hull shapes, and therefore less wetted area, have an advantage at slow speeds, because the friction resistance can be up to 70 per cent of the overall resistance. In addition, boat 2 copes better with wind pressure and choppy seas and cuts better into the water because of the pointed hull shape. A coefficient of between 5.0 and 6.0 indicates good all-round qualities. You should look for a cruising yacht that has such coefficients; variances between the boat being slightly lighter or a little bit heavier are acceptable.

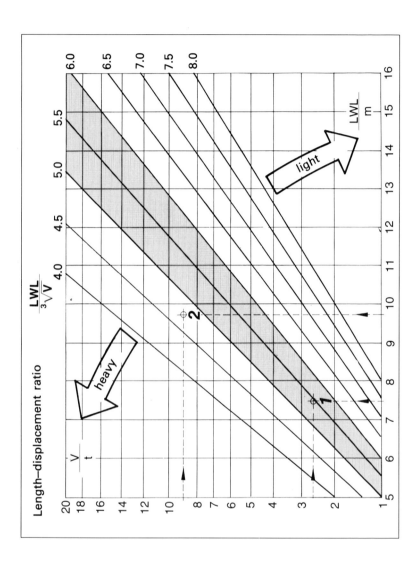

Fig 31 (Opposite) The waterline in relation to the displacement displays a yacht's weight in relation to the waterline. Modern yachts are between 5.0 and 6.0; heavy yachts below 5.0 and light displacement yachts can have coefficients of up to 8.0. In order to determine this coefficient, take the displacement from the vertical axis to the right and the LWL from the horizontal axis to the top. The intersection of the two lines will tell you whether you are dealing with a relatively heavy or light boat.

Sail area–displacement ratio

The question of whether the boat is over- or under-canvased is answered in Fig 32 (sail area–displacement ratio). The displacement is applied on to the sail area: $\sqrt{AS}/3\sqrt{V}$. The coefficients state the potential forward drive in relation to the boat's displacement (weight). The intersection of the sail area applied to the horizontal axis, and the displacement weight applied to the vertical axis, indicates the tendency of the sail area–displacement ratio. In old technical books, this relationship is known as the sail-carrying number and the size of the sail area is dependent upon the displacement. The lines allow a judgement of how fast a boat sails in medium winds. The higher the value, the more potential drive the yacht has.

A large sail area (AS) with a high displacement (V) can produce the same value as a small sail area with a low displacement. A large sail area with high displacement is faster in light winds. A large sail area is not important in strong winds, as you will have to reef down. Canvasing values with coefficients between 3.8 and 5.0 are normal. This is where most of the cruising yachts lie. Boat 1 in Fig 32 would be over-canvased, while boat 2 could be called normal. These days, not even motorsailers are under-canvased.

Sail area–length ratio

Is my boat fast or slow? The coefficient that brings the sail area into relationship with the LWL ($\sqrt{AS}/LWL$) displays the

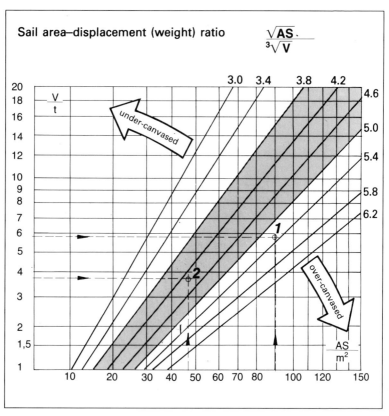

Fig 32 The sail area in relation to the displacement produces a so-called sail-carrying number, ie whether a yacht carries a relatively large or small sail area. Yachts with present-day canvasing achieve coefficients between 3.8 and 5.0. Boats with a coefficient of less than 3.8 are under-canvased, those with more than 5.0 are over-canvased. The sail-carrying number can be obtained from the diagram by applying the displacement from the vertical axis to the right, and the sail area from the horizontal axis to the top.

forward drive of the boat in relation to her length. The boat-builder's saying 'Length runs' is related to the yacht's effective waterline, ie her hull speed. If a yacht is to achieve her hull speed she requires sufficient sail area. A high sail area–length coefficient indicates sufficient sail, which uses the given waterline efficiently. For this, coefficients of 0.8 to 1.0 are generally required. Values below this indicate too slow a displacement, which is rarely found these days; values above (boat 1 in Fig 33) describe a fast displacement yacht.

Sailing speed–waterline ratio

How fast can a boat sail as a consequence of its waterline length? The answer can be obtained by applying its LWL in metres and its speed in knots ($V^s/\sqrt{LWL}$). Heavy boats with pure displacement lines require a sail area of 8 to 12 square metres per ton of boat in order to achieve speeds of 2.43 $\sqrt{LWL}$. The average cruiser achieves speeds of 1.63 $\sqrt{LWL}$. Only a larger sail area allows higher performance. An increase in speed is possible first through larger sail areas, ie more stability, and second, with a smaller length–displacement ratio (Figs 31 and 32). In such cases, heavy displacement yachts can achieve speeds of up to 2.72 $\sqrt{LWL}$, and light displacements of up to 3.62. Only ultralights (extremely light designs) and dinghies will eventually achieve planing conditions, and thus achieve speeds of 4.88 $\sqrt{LWL}$ (as measured on a Flying Dutchman).

The speed–waterline coefficient clarifies the fact that high speeds can only be counted on where there is a large waterline length, because there are few extremely light cruising yachts. Fig 33 offers a quick overview of the speed you can expect from a given boat.

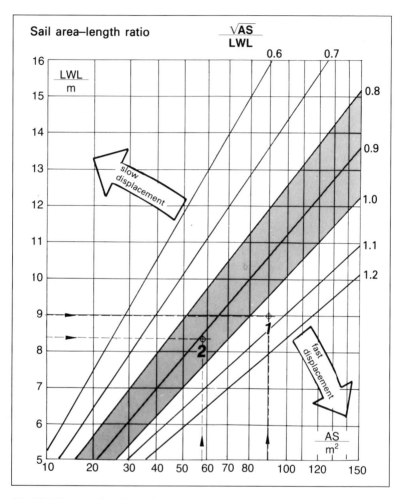

Fig 33 The relationship of a boat's sail area to waterline length indicates the dependency of a yacht's speed on the LWL. Therefore, you can have a fast or a slow displacement. The higher the coefficient, the faster the boat. The intersection of the length of the waterline from the vertical axis to the right, and the sail area from the horizontal axis to the top, tells you whether a yacht sails relatively fast or slow in comparison to other boats.

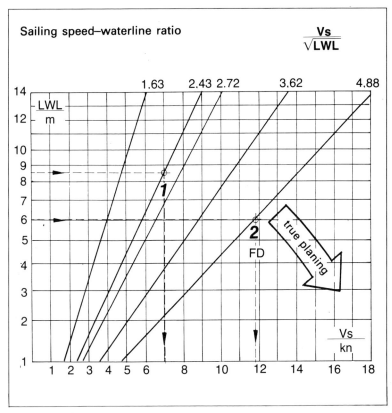

Fig 34 If you put the boat's speed into relationship with the waterline, it results in the Froude's value, a figure that indicates the boat's speed. Accordingly, the number 1.6 indicates the average performance of a cruiser. 2.43 is the factor for the wave speed, according to the hull speed. Heavy yachts can reach a maximum of 2.72, light displacement yachts up to a value of 3.62. After this, you reach the planing condition, which is value 4.88. In order to determine a yacht's speed, you apply the LWL from the vertical axis to the right until the suitable line is reached: 2.43 for heavy, 2.72 for lighter yachts, 3.62 for ultralight yachts. The vertical line from this intersection to the horizontal Vs-axis produces the expected boat speed in knots.

7 Evaluating diagrams at home

Each ratio-factor makes a statement about each individual characteristic of a boat. A diagram with the parameters waterline length, sail area and displacement puts the three most important factors for a yacht's performance into relationship: the coefficients of Figs 31, 32 and 33 result in the diagram for the sailing performance:

$$\sqrt{AS}/LWL \times LWL/^3\sqrt{V} = \sqrt{AS}/^3\sqrt{V}$$

Another diagram, although quite unconventional, represents the attempt to represent a yacht's characteristics in such a way that the viewer will see them at first glance. Everybody can draw the required sketches.

Sailing performance diagram

A yacht's performance depends on several factors. Its LWL, AS and V are easily determined. Using figures from brochures you can compare the speed to be expected in comparison to that of others by using the sailing performance diagram. This is a lot more realistic than comparing boats purely by their hull speed, as it is generally as valuable as sailing the boats against each other. The theoretical comparison is based on the LWL. On downwind courses with strong winds, the LWL becomes the only speed-limiting factor apart from the rigging. High proportional values of a boat's sail area to her waterline stand for an optimal exploitation; applied to the vertical axis of the co-ordinate system in Fig 35. Another important factor for a boat's speed is the displacement as already seen in the corresponding coefficients. The length–displacement as a measure for the distributed weight on the waterline was applied on to the horizontal axis of the co-ordinate system. The only thing missing is the third factor, the relation of the sail area towards the displacement. This so-called sail-carrying ability of a yacht reappears again as a ladder of lines (from the bottom left to the top right).

This diagram allows you to determine the sailing performance of any yacht. The higher a boat climbs up the lines because of characteristic features, the faster it will sail in medium wind conditions. The vertical axis indicates when a yacht is fast because of a large sail area and the horizontal axis indicates whether the boat achieves high speeds as a result of light construction. Therefore, you find fast boats at the top right and slow boats to the bottom left; heavy ones on the left, under-canvased boats at the bottom. A good all-rounder will always be in the middle of the co-ordinate system. You can also see from the diagram whether you are dealing with a boat that is good in light winds like (boat 1 in Fig 35) or whether the boat requires more wind (like boat 2 in Fig 35). Boat 3 in this figure displays the best all-round qualities. You will find great similarity if you compare the theoretical values with actual sailing values. Yacht designers proceed the same way: they just do it the other way around.

For the test sails that will follow, the future buyer will in any case already know which probable qualities his trial boat has: he should not even bother to set sail in light winds if the boat reads 'bottom right' in Fig 35.

Qualities at a glance

The famous yacht builder and draughtsman Robert Das developed a drawing technique (published 1966 in the magazine *Yacht*) that allows direction comparisons of yachts in order to detect a yacht's characteristics at first glance. It is based on basic physical laws and has been refined through experience. You draw the boat's hull (best scale 1:50) consisting of LOA and LWL with a freeboard of 0.1 LWL (as seen in Fig 36). You then draw a so-called breadth-circle with half of the BWL (always use the same scale) and a displacement circle with $0.5^3\sqrt{V}$. You can enter the proportion of ballast in degrees (ballast in relation to the displacement) in this circle. The luff

Sailing performance diagram

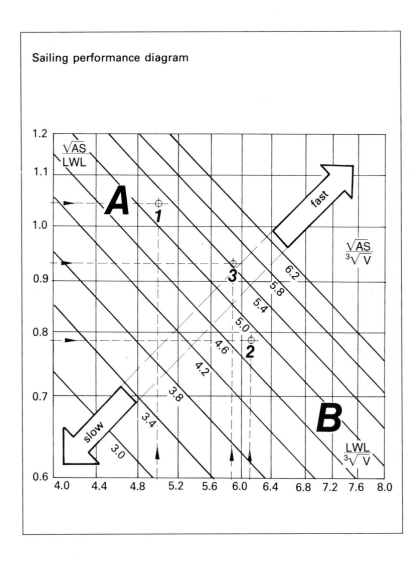

Fig 35 (Opposite) This sailing performance diagram contains the factors that determine a boat's speed, ie the length of the waterline (LWL), the sail area (AS) and the displacement (V). A boat's speed can be calculated by using the relational values $LWL/_3\sqrt{V}$ and $\sqrt{AS}/LWL$. From the vertical axis to the right and the horizontal axis to the top, the intersection of both lines displays the potential speed. A boat that can be found in the top-right section of the diagram is therefore the faster one, conditional upon medium winds. In relation to its waterline, it has the largest sail area and the smallest displacement. Yachts in section A are fair-weather yachts (large sail area with high displacement), yachts in section B can cope with stronger winds (less displacement, small sail area).

of the sail is drawn from the front with a distance of 1/3 LWL.

Its length I is produced by 2 x $0.75\sqrt{AS}$ for the sail area; the factor 0.75 for the main sail is only there for optical reasons. The foot of the sail is entered with its simple length of $0.75\sqrt{AS}$. The tangent A is drawn from the edge of the LWL to the breadth-circle and tangent B on to the displacement circle. The Robert Das 'Boat Comparison' is as simple as that!

The sail area-triangle denotes whether a yacht is over- or under-canvased or whether the rig is balanced. If the leach of the symbolic sail cuts off with the waterline, her canvasing is suitable for medium wind and sea conditions. The two smaller diagrams show an over-canvased boat (**I**) and an under-canvased boat (**II**).

The line A (tangent to the breadth-circle) gives a rough impression of the waves. The size of the angle with which it runs aft is determined by the boat's beam. Therefore, line A permits rough estimations with regard to the yacht's speed (shallow tangent). It also denotes whether it is narrow or wide, because the more acute the angle, the slimmer the boat.

Line B as a tangent on the displacement circle displays the relationship of the boat's waterline length to its displacement. It is therefore an indication as to whether the boat is heavy or light, and subsequently determines the possibility of planing. According to Fig 36, speeds above $2.43\sqrt{LWL}$ are not possible if line B is below the waterline. Experience has shown that a

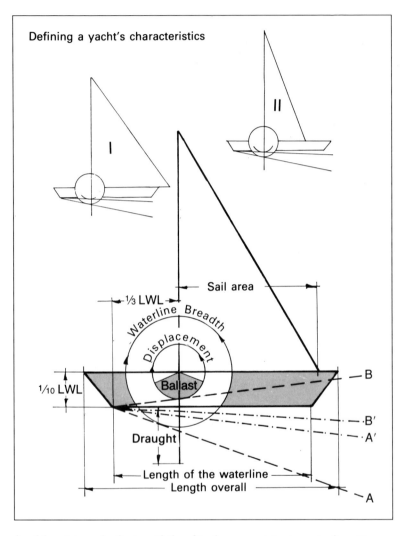

Defining a yacht's characteristics

keel boat is only faster if the displacement in tons is five times or more the waterline in metres.

Of course, a yacht drawn in this symbolic way does not constitute a constructional plan. It is purely for the purpose of comparing boats and simultaneously displaying them optically.

Fig 36 (Opposite) After drawing the diagram to scale, levelling the sail area and applying the displacement- and breadth-circle (according to the construction description), you can read the following characteristics: 1) large sail-triangle (as in **I**) – over-canvased, 2) small sail-triangle (**II**) – under-canvased, 3) shallow tangent A – fast boat (the more shallow, the faster), 4) steep tangent A' – slow boat (the steeper, the slower), 5) tangent B above the waterline – light displacement, 6) tangent B' below the waterline – heavy displacement. It also depends on the relationship of AS, V and LWL.

8 Performance details: trials on the water

If you want to get to know a yacht properly you have to sail it. Everything that has been said so far serves simply to assist the evaluation of a yacht without actually experiencing the performance underway. To sail the yacht eventually is the icing on the cake. With your acquired theoretical knowledge, you will evaluate the boat with your eyes open because you can predetermine some of the characteristics and will therefore experience them more intensively in practice. Whether you change your mind about characteristics that you theoretically determined as negative when you actually sail the yacht is another thing. The important thing is to combine theory and practice.

Under sail

To understand a yacht's characteristics such as good speed, height to windward, manoeuvrability and so on, is something that requires experience and time. Seldom can you lay your hands on 'trial boats' for a long enough period, be it at boat shows, in their element, or in boatyards. Nine times out of ten there are other customers aboard with you, so that the trial sail is handled by somebody from the boatyard or yacht broker who is familiar with the boat. You therefore need to plan some standard manoeuvres that will reveal the yacht's character even over a limited period of time.

Speed

If you want to establish a boat's potential speed, in practice you will need a compass and a speedometer. Nowadays, these instruments are standard equipment. Sometimes, the wind makes it more difficult: with a sufficient amount of sail it has to blow strongly enough for a boat to reach hull speed on an offwind course. You can recognise this on the waves behind the stern; the wake runs smoothly without turbulence from the lower transom. This is when the boat sails at $2.43\sqrt{LWL}$ knots.

If you compare this speed with that of the speedometer, it produces a correction factor of 1 if true speed and speed of the speedometer are equal. For different speeds, the correction factor is produced from the quotient $V_{true}/V_{speedometer}$, ie from the true speed divided by the speed measured. The speed indicator is therefore not gauged (differences might be slightly variable for other courses and speeds), but it is sufficient for the test. Now you sail three courses: close to the wind, 90 degrees off the wind, and downwind, whereby you need to notice whether an increase in speed is due to a gust or whether the helmsman has fallen off his course. Those three average speeds already display a yacht's potential speed. If you follow the same procedure in lighter winds or in the same wind force but reefed, you will find out about the boat's qualities in fair weather.

If you are lucky and the wind increases, you can also check out the qualities in heavy going; a good all-round boat should be able to carry her 'windward canvas' with ease up to a force 4.

You can also draw a so-called apple-diagram with the speeds of the three courses. More courses would obviously be better. If you assume that the speed of an average boat differentiates by 1 knot between sailing close-hauled (45 degrees) and on a beam reach (90 degrees) and by a maximum of 2 knots between a downwind leg (180 degrees) and a broad reach (135 degrees), you will have two extra points for this polar diagram.

Height to windward

You can easily determine your height to windward by using the compass when tacking: you measure the tacking angle of about five tacks. Divided by two, it will give you your height to

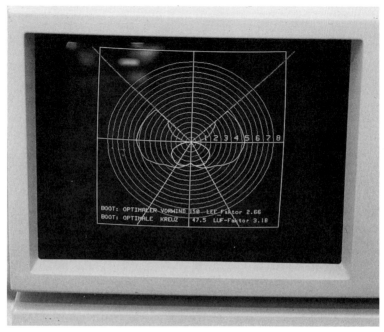

These days, polar diagrams are drawn by computer. Only three main courses are generally required: close-hauled, beam reach and downwind. The optimum course to windward and downwind, together with their subsequent speeds made good, are produced simultaneously. With the monitor aboard, you only need to re-enact the optimum course.

windward. It generally lies between 38 and 45 degrees, whereby the smaller angle is for slim boats with a good keel profile (also for a pointed long-keeler), and the higher degrees are for broad motorsailers. All other boat types are somewhere in between.

The optimum height to windward, ie the angle to the true wind, which lies between extreme pinching and acceptable forward drive, can be obtained from the polar diagram: it displays visibly how much the boat speed reduces with increasing height to windward. The optimum angle of height is obtained by applying a horizontal tangent to the boat's speed curve (polar diagram).

Ultimate speed to windward

Measuring the speed of a yacht to windward does not depend on the maximum speed, what is important is ultimate speed made good to windward (as you can read from the polar diagram after applying the tangent). On board a yacht you can obtain the final speed, $V_{windward}$, by reading the boat's speed through the water V_{speed} and simultaneously determine the course angle towards the true wind. By definition, it is the product from speed and cosine of the course angle.

The same applies to the ultimate speed downwind: it also pays to tack in front of the wind (to prevent sailing by the lee). A lot of sailing instruments already calculate speed and course angle on board, so that you might be able to read the final speed of your trial boat. A good performance to windward will be shown by a yacht with a high speed made good to windward at a given speed of the true wind V_W. The larger the ratio $V_{windward}$ /V_{wind}, the greater are (for example) the chances of success on a triangular course and the more effective – regarding the lateral force – is the keel and rudder, not to mention the sails!

Turning circle

A good option for displaying a boat's manoeuvrability is to turn a circle: from a windward course with maximum speed you put the rudder across without handling the sails and then check the time. Light boats with narrow fin keels and free hung spade rudders require between 20 and 30 seconds, a fin-keeler with skeg in front of the rudder requires between 30 and 40 seconds, and heavy boats with long keels require between 40 and 60 seconds.

A design problem that occurs over and over again when turning a circle is to find a boat that is highly manoeuvrable and at the same time highly stable. All compromises are somewhere in between. Another factor that appears when turning a circle is the effect of the rudder: if the vertical rotating axis of the hull (usually shortly behind the front edge of the keel) and the rudder's point of effort are too close together, the boat reacts sluggishly.

A lot of wind and boat speed indicators also display the speed made good to windward (VMG). This combined instrument from Silva shows both.

Leeway

A good indication of the effectiveness of the keel and the rudder against the lateral force of the water is the boat's leeway. The less leeway a boat has the better. For an exact determination of a boat's speed and true course with induced and true wind, the leeway is as important as the speed made good to windward. Measuring the leeway is quite difficult. You would need to measure in front and far behind the boat in undisturbed water. At the moment, you have the option of determining the leeway by estimating (or taking a bearing) the angle of the boat's stern wake to her longitudinal axis. A small angle signifies sufficient lateral area with good height to windward. With large angles you have to be careful when mooring the boat as it tends to drift sideways.

Heeling

In past years it was quite normal for yachts to heel up to the gunwales – even in relatively light winds. Boats with large overhangs (Skerry cruisers or Dragons) are designed to sail heeled, as it elongates the waterline. Modern, wide fin-keelers follow the contrary concept; their lines are perfect if the boat can be sailed upright. Their speed can only be maintained by

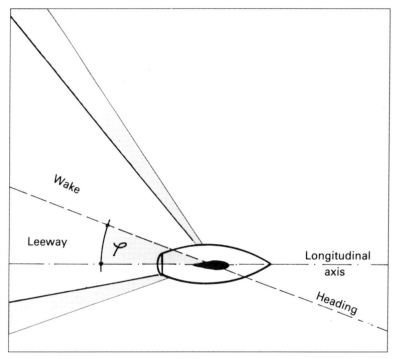

Fig 37 A boat's leeway is difficult to establish. One option is to esti-mate the angle between the longitudinal axis of the boat and her wake.

reefing early. Too much heeling makes the boat unbalanced and difficult to manoeuvre because the rudder comes out of the water too easily.

If you want to avoid spending all your time sitting on the windward side of the boat as a cruising sailor, the boat will need sufficient stiffness. You can already recognise the stiff-ness of a boat if you step on to the side of a 10 metre yacht. Whether a yacht is tender or stiff is irrelevant to stability as the ballast only becomes effective with increased heeling. Modern cruisers have to put a reef in when the boat is heeled only at about 30 degrees, while slimmer long cut-away keelers can continue to sail up to a heeling angle of about 50 degrees.

Sailing performance by comparative values

Why can't a computer come up with a quick estimation of a yacht's sailing performance? In fact, there is a computer that does just this. Microelectronics have presented a large selection of measuring devices for yacht navigation, but no matter how good they are, once on board these wind- and water-measuring devices are subject to a series of errors. For example, a variable stream flow during the different courses, the boats yawing and rolling movements at the log, heeling and upwards movement of the air flow due to the sail at the wind indicator are just a few such errors.

Dr Eng H Brandt, Professor of Hydrodynamics at the Technical University in Berlin, has developed a calculation method that allows comparisons to be made between similar boats, and that produces a yacht's sailing performance by means of a performance-ratio. For this you need details of the boat's LWL, BWL, sail area and displacement, as are also required in the sailing performance diagram (Fig 35). You also enter two additional correction factors in the computer: these are resistance and sail quality. The program calculates sailing performance, together with the measured values of the log and wind indicator, that is not limited to the determination of the currently sailed speed to windward. It also includes the theoretical boat speed of a comparative boat with identical initial data for boat speed, wind angle and leeway.

As an added feature, you will get additional values for the resistance and forward drive, whose data have been collected in a series of lengthy measuring tests. The computer program considers the aerodynamic force of the sails, the sail-carrying ability, ie the yacht's stability, and the complete range of resistances such as towing and wind resistance, leeway and heeling. The aim of a sailing performance calculation is that the forward drive corresponds to the yacht's hydrodynamic resistance and therefore produces a theoretical boat speed. This computer is built by the German instrument manufacturer VDO, but can it replace personal evaluation and intuition?

Under engine

As harbours and marinas become more crowded, it is important to manoeuvre under engine, because in most cases you will not be able to come alongside or cast off under sail. You have to use your engine in order to park the boat in a narrow mooring slot. It also helps to be able to overcome a lull and stem a tide.

Whether a sailing yacht benefits from an engine depends as much on performance and the propeller fitted as on the optimal thrust on the rudder. Changes can easily be made if the diameter of the prop is not geared to the engine's performance and its rotating speed is not suited to the boat's speed. It becomes more difficult if the prop is situated too far away from the rudder. You need to do a major refit if the rudder blade is to be brought into the prop's thrust.

Speed

Your engine should have two speeds, top speed and cruising speed. Auxiliary propulsion's first priority should be to achieve the boat's hull speed, the second should be that it works quietly, economically and without vibration. It is suggested that yachts that sail in open seas have a 10–20 per cent performance reserve. Often, the hull speed is not reached, which is largely the result of an incorrect angle of the folding prop rather than the engine's performance. However, a folding prop has less resistance when sailing in comparison to a fixed prop. Tests in the experimental tank have shown that speed loss is only 0.01 knots at a speed of 5 knots for folding props, while a fixed prop reaches values of 0.8 knots.

The cruising speed is generally defined as 80 per cent of the top speed. The boat is sailed on the rev-counter and either measured with a verified log or by sailing a measured mile: course and reciprocal course divided by two in order to eliminate winds and current. Remember, 1 knot is 1 sea mile per hour!

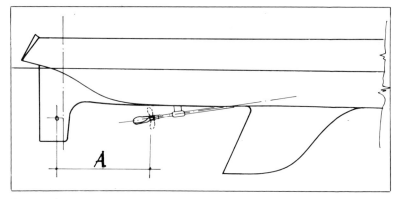

Fig 38 So that the rudder gets the optimum thrust from the propeller, distance A should be as small as possible. Otherwise, the result is poor manoeuvrability under engine.

Turning circle and reverse drive

A good way to establish a yacht's manoeuvrability under engine is to turn a circle. You drive the boat to starboard and port with cruising speed (80 per cent of full speed) and check the time it requires to complete the circle. If you turn the boat to port, it generally requires less time because most boats have right-handed props that reinforce the waterflow to the rudder. Turning times between 10 and 30 seconds are acceptable for a yacht. The higher value is more for the cut-away keeler.

The diameter of the circle should not exceed 1½–2 boat lengths. Everything above this requires an inspection of the rudder and propeller. If, for example, a wave comes out straight behind the fin, the rudder of the fin-keeler often does not get enough thrust from the propeller because it is situated too far away, while the propeller may possibly prevent a good stream thrust in a long-keeler. Boats like this can only be manoeuvred with a lot of speed in crowded harbours. An indication of good manoeuvrability is always if the boat's rudder handles well when reversing. Front-balanced free-hanging rudders are very effective in this case, although dangerous: if the push backward is too large, it easily rips the tiller from the helmsman as it directly oversteers. A rudder with a skeg is friendlier to handle, although not as effective as the spade rudder. A yacht has good manoeuvrability if it can be reversed into the mooring slot. If the rudder-to-propeller alignment is correct, it will be easier to reverse the boat because boats steer with their sterns.

Stopway

Though a yacht has no brake as such, it should at least be able to stop in reasonable time. The loss of way – or stopway – indicates what period of time is required before you have to reverse in order to cease to make headway at a certain point. For this, you drive the boat at cruising speed (80 per cent full speed) and check the time between reversing and standstill.

The complete process must be measured in calm water with wind and waves on the beam. The time measured for light boats with a large propeller is between 8 and 12 seconds, for heavy boats or boats with folding props, it is up to 20 seconds or more. The formula $0.26 \times v \times t$ produces the stopway; v is the boat speed in knots and t the time in seconds. The factor of 0.26 is to convert knots into metres, so that the total loss of way is given in metres. A yacht should not require more than two boat lengths in order to stop. Anything above this results in difficulty in manoeuvring.

Stability and metacentric height

First-time buyers in particular are always anxious as to whether the boat is self-righting. With keel boats, the answer is generally 'Yes'. However, the location and amount of ballast carried will affect the stability, and also the behaviour in a seaway: too much righting moment will produce a jerky motion as the hull first heels, then abruptly comes upright. A comfortable cruiser should have only sufficient ballast to ensure that inversion is all but impossible, but not so much as to impart a violent motion in a seaway. Two relatively simple tests display a given boat's stability in relation to other well-known designs.

Boatbuilders use the word stable for the balanced condition of the complete boat. A yacht's safety is the heeling stability that allows it to return upright from extreme angles. A measure of stability is defined as the metacentric height GM, the distance between the metacentre and centre of gravity (see chapter 'The yacht itself' – 'stability'). It takes considerable effort to calculate the stability, and brochures do not offer all the required details.

There are two methods for the practical interpretation of GM, both of which are easy to perform even on a yacht that is already afloat. In method 1 the yacht is heeled on a calm day with all equipment, ie gear, crew and half-filled tanks. The boat is tied loosely to the mooring and a weight is placed on to the sidedeck and shifted from the middle towards the side (you can use the crew!), so that the boat heels visibly. The measuring device for the heeling angle is a pendulum that is installed below deck (string with a small weight). The metacentric height in metres is obtained by using the heeling weight m (about 150 kg for a 10 metre yacht), the length of the shifting way on deck e, the swing of the pendulum s, the length of the pendulum l and the displacement of the yacht V:

$$GM = \frac{m_k \times e \times l}{V \times s}$$

The other method is even more simple: you measure the yacht's rolling time. For this, you heel the boat and measure the time that the top of the mast requires to complete a swing from one side to the other. If several swings are measured, the result becomes more accurate. When the GM is calculated, the result has to be divided by the number of swings. The formula is:

$$GM = \frac{(B_{max} \times C)}{T} 2$$

B_{max} is the largest breadth in metres, T the swinging time in seconds (one swing represents the natural swing of the

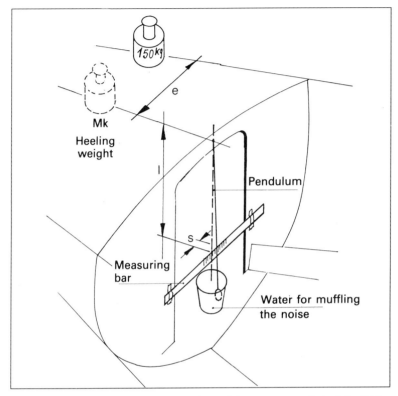

Fig 39 Heeling test for determination of the metacentric height GM:
You measure the length of the pendulum l, its swing s, and the shifting way e. The heeling weight can be made up by crew members.

yacht), C is a factor for differentiating between heavy and
light yachts (1.56 for heavy and 1.24 for light; other boats are
somewhere in between). Depending on the yacht's stability,
you measure between 4 and 16 seconds for her natural swing.
Both formulas are approximate and are valid for the initial
stability, ie for heeling angles up to about 15 degrees.

Stability comparison

A yacht's metacentric height on its own does not reveal anything. The lever curve is missing, and this, in most cases, is not obtainable. You can help yourself by comparing the stability of other yachts. Designers use an empirically established value, the Dellenbough-coefficient, because even for them the calculation of the displacement's centre of effort and the waterline's momentum of inertia for each heeling angle is quite long-winded. The Dellenbough-coefficient (DC) indicates a yacht's heeling angle close-hauled in a force 4 with the wind diagonal to the heading (equivalent to a wind pressure on the

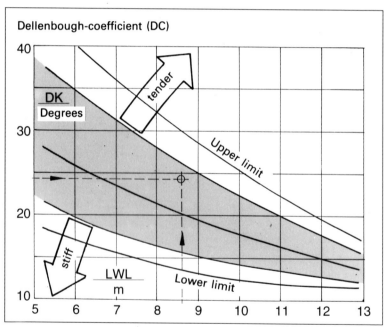

Fig 40 The Dellenbough-coefficient (DC) allows conclusions concerning a yacht's stability. With the aid of a diagram, the calculated value serves as a comparison. The DC value applied from the vertical and the waterline length from the horizontal axis provides an intersection that indicates whether a boat is stiff or tender.

sail of 4.88daN/m^2). The value is only useful if you are able to make comparisons. These are available with the aid of a diagram (Fig 40). It shows the DC-values applied above the waterline, which have been established from IOR-rating certificates of the German Sailing Association (DSV). The calculated coefficient and the waterline offer a good impression of a yacht's stability. The Dellenbough-coefficient is calculated as follows:

$$DC = \frac{p \times AS \times (H + 0.4\ T)}{GM \times V}$$

The wind pressure p is thereby equivalent to 4.88 daN/m^2, the sail area AS in square metres, the sails' centre of effort H above the WL in metres, the draught T in metres, the metacentric height GM in metres, and the displacement in kg. The result is the DC in degrees.

The Dellenbough-coefficient is the practical counterpart of the sail-carrying number made up from the sail area and displacement, which also indicates the comparative value as to whether a yacht is tender or stiff. Additionally, it gives rough details about the type of boat. The metacentric height of an upright position is used. It does not consider the additional influence of the shape.

Appendix

Symbols and terms

International

LOA	[m]	Length overall, or the length of the hull; jib boom or free hung rudders not included.
LWL	[m]	Length of the general waterline. Because of different displacements – empty or full – boatbuilders state the LWL together with the corresponding draught, eg LWL 1.8 with 1.6 m draught.
B	[m]	Breadth of the outer edge of the outer skin.
BWL	[m]	Breadth of the waterline.
T	[m]	Largest draught.
TR	[m]	Moulded draught of shallow cruisers or boats without keel.
TS	[m]	Draught of centreboard.
F	[m]	Freeboard.
FV	[m]	Freeboard at the bow.
FH	[m]	Freeboard at the stern.
FM	[m]	Freeboard on boats of 0.5 LOA or boats with a seam at their lowest point.
V ∇	[m³]	Displacement in the water, ie volume of the underwater hull regarding her outer skin.
D $\triangle$	[t]	Displacement in tonnage = weight of the water displaced in sea water, ie fully equipped yacht inclusive of crew, effects, provisions and tanks. $D(t) = D(w) \times \rho$ ($\rho = 1.025$)
BA	[t]	Ballast in kg or tons, but not in percentages as it can cause great differences – especially in small boats (full or empty).
AS	[m²]	Sail area, ie the largest effective sail area to windward (mainsail and 150% genoa, where the genoa overlaps by 50%). Individual sails are identified by numbers that occur in the sail plan, ie AS 1, 1 = mainsail, 2 = 150% genoa, 3 = mizzen, 4 = balloon jib, etc with individual determination.

AM   [m^2]   Midship section area, in comparison to the boatbuilding, the maximum cross-section is measured which is mostly outside of 0.5 LWL.

AK   [m^2]   Profile area of the keel.

AR   [m^2]   Profile area of the rudder.

AW   [m^2]   Waterline area.

S   [m^2]   Wetted surface (unrolled) of the hull, including keel and rudder profile (not unrolled).

ALP   [m^2]   Overall lateral area, ie hull, keel and rudder profile (not unrolled)

CWP α Volume degree of the waterline area

$$\frac{AW}{L \times B}$$

CM β Volume degree of the midship section area (excluding the keel).

M   Metacentre.

MB   [m]   Metacentric height, ie height of the breadth-metacentre above the displacement centre of effort.

MG   [m]   Metacentric height, ie height of the breadth-metacentre above the displacement (tonnage) centre of effort (G).

PHI φ [°]   Heeling angle, also shown as φ.

h   [m]   Lever of the static stability.

MST   [Nm]   General stability momentum.

MKR   [Nm]   Heeling momentum.

MAR   [Nm]   Uprighting momentum.

SM   [Nm/°]   Sailing momentum. MAR = MKR with the heeling angle 'Water on deck' with the sail area AS (main + 150% genoa).

IE   [°]   Entry angle of the waterline, ie angle between the waterline and the midship area on the bow.

IR   [°]   Exit angle of the waterline, ie angle between the midship area on the stern.

B   Displacement centre of effort, general.

G   Centre of gravity.

CS   Coefficient of the wetted surface

$$CS = \frac{S}{\sqrt{V \times L}}$$

CSA | Ratio of the sail area to the wetted surface

$$CSA = \frac{AS}{S}$$

CLP | Lateral plan coefficient

$$CLP = \frac{ALP}{LWL \times T}$$

CDL | Displacement-to-length ratio

$$CDL = \frac{D}{(0.1 \times LWL)^3}$$

CLV | Length-to-displacement ratio

$$CLV = \frac{LWL}{\sqrt[3]{V}}$$

CDL and CLV are similar, but the latter is to be preferred because of dimension equality. In England, the CDL-values are better known.

CAV | Sail area-to-displacement ratio

$$CAV = \frac{\sqrt{AS}}{\sqrt[3]{V}}$$

Vo [m/s] | Boat speed.

FN | Froude-value

$$FN = \frac{V}{\sqrt{g \times LWL} \; (g = 9.81)}$$

VS [kn] | Boat speed.

R | Relative speed

$$R = \frac{V}{\sqrt{LWL}} \; (\frac{kn}{m})$$

Generally common in English-speaking countries and with sailors (eg as hull speed with Vo = 2.43 $\sqrt{LWL}$). Engineers and scientists prefer to use the Froude-value.

RP $[\frac{1}{T}]$ | Rolling period

$$GM = (\frac{f \times B}{T})^2$$

If the GM is known, you can establish the

f-values for determining the boat's stability if you have sufficient readings/measurements.

DKR $\left[\frac{1}{T}\right]$ Measurement of the turning circle in 360 degrees in metres and the time in seconds.

L:B Length towards breadth, preferably values of the waterline, ie LWL:BWL.

B:T Breadth towards draught, preferably values of the waterline, ie BWL:T.

Beaufort Wind Scale

No	General description	Wind speed (knots)	Sea state
0	Calm	Less than 1	Sea like a mirror
1	Light air	1–3	Ripples: no foam crests in open sea
2	Light breeze	4–6	Small wavelets with crests that do not break
3	Gentle breeze	7–10	Large wavelets; crests begin to break: some white horses
4	Moderate breeze	11–16	Longer waves with white horses
5	Fresh breeze	17–21	Moderate waves; many white horses; some spray
6	Strong breeze	22–27	Large waves with white foam crests; spray
7	Near gale	28–33	Sea heaps up; white foam blown in streaks
8	Gale	34–40	Moderately high waves; some spindrift: visible foam streaks
9	Strong gale	41–47	High waves; crests begin to topple and tumble; dense foam streaks; spray affects visibility
10	Storm	48–55	Very high waves with crests: sea surface becomes almost white; visibility affected
11	Violent storm	56–63	Exceptionally high waves; sea covered in foam; visibility badly affected
12	Hurricane	64+	Air filled with foam and spray; sea white; visibility seriously affected

Reading lines plans

Though there are still individually built yachts, most these days are factory-produced. Their hulls are made from a mould, which is used for all subsequent hulls. A lines plan is only required for production of the mould. In spite of this, the resultant cast shows the lines that characterise the yacht's hull. At boat shows, if one looked at hulls whose shapes would be eligible for industrial design awards, it would be those with the most eye-catching lines plans. A lines plan's detailed information regarding a boat's hull is much better than looking at a photo. Very often you get more information about a yacht's character by looking at the lines plan than if you saw the vessel standing on land. Even if you walk around the boat, you will not see all the qualities as well as if you studied a plan.

With a little bit of practice, you will soon develop a feeling for the beautiful lines of a yacht. Except for IOR hulls, all lines run smoothly without bumps and dents. Boatbuilders in Germany say 'A line strakes'. This derives from the low German and means 'stroking'. If you watch how a wooden hull is cleaned and polished you soon understand the meaning: the boatbuilder runs his hand over the hull in order to recognise uneven lines that do not 'strake' – or, to put it another way, are not fair.

The lines should strake so that the water flow glides along the yacht when sailing and does not produce resistance through turbulence. This leads to the conclusion that a good straking yacht is also a fast yacht, and because more yachts today are built to sail fast by lessening displacement; a heavy yacht with a smooth underwater line is at least not slow. You will understand this if you look at the lines plans of older boats (very rarely will you be able to see plans of newer factory-built boats). A trained eye will soon be able to differentiate and this will make the choice of the right boat simpler.

A yacht's lines are curved, not straight, and both halves of the hull must be exactly symmetrical and have equally straking lines if the performance is to be acceptable. This requires an accurate drawing plan whose measurements are later scaled up. In times when such design was not computer-aided, at least the strake was correct because the points on the drawing were connected by using a strake batten that only permits fair lines and curves. A plotter, in comparison, does not realise if a curve is too sharp or whether a line has a bump. Sometimes, in any case, bumps and dents are actually required, so that the boats conform to the IOR ratings.

The lines plan displays hulls from three different angles: longitudinal elevation, horizontal section and profile. In the longitudinal and horizontal section the bow is always on the right and the after part always to the left; the horizontal section and the profile generally display only one-half of the boat, while the other half is the mirror image. In order to obtain a complete drawing plan, the hull is cut open several times in different directions. The borderlines of these cuts are curves that are known as sections, waterlines, cuts and centrelines.

Sections are created when the hull is cut into equal slices (cross-sections) from the stern to the bow. The largest section is the midship section. Because it is so important, both port and starboard sides are displayed. On the right of the centreline are the sections of the forepart, on the left those of the stern. The profile section of the drawing plan is the section. Here, the sections are shown as straight lines. The lines are numbered consecutively from aft from 0 onwards.

Waterlines are shown when the hull is cut into horizontal slices. The borderlines are the waterlines. The upper part of the horizontal plan represents the waterline section. The most important waterline is the construction waterline CWL. It is the calculated waterline on which the boat should float. Because the underwater hull is mostly responsible for a yacht's performance, the waterlines are taken at closer intervals.

Cuts are for checking the section and waterlines; longitudinal sections are placed parallel to the midship area and these divide the hull into perpendicular slices. These curves are found again in the longitudinal plan.

Centrelines are cuts taken from the midship area, so that

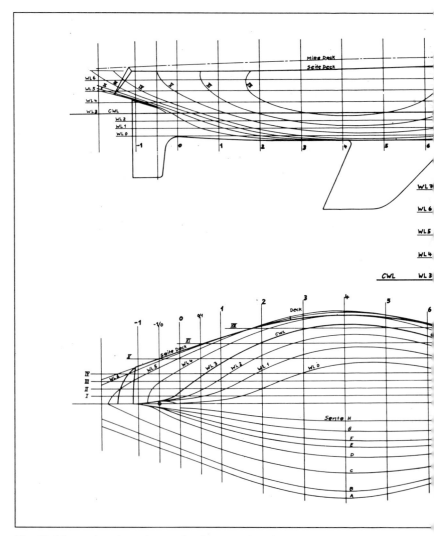

Fig 41 Lines plan: In order to display a yacht's hull two-dimensionally, you require sections that cut the body into slices: vertical sections longitudinally (I to VII) produce the longitudinal section (above), horizontal cuts (WL0 to WL7) the waterlines (below) and vertical cuts of the intersection (-1 to 10) display the midship section. The numbers in the profile display the series of the sections.

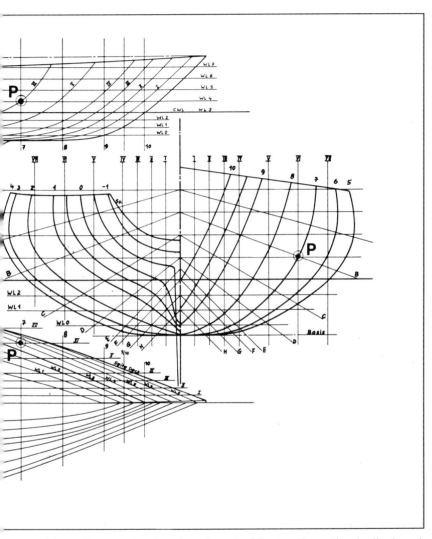

You will recognise that the left part of the boat's section is displayed from aft (section -1 to 4) and the right part is from the front (section 5 to 10). Section 4 is the midship section. The diagonal sections (A to H) are the centrelines. These sections determine every point on the outer skin. They recur in all three displays. Example P:7/VI/WL4.

as many sections as possible are cut vertically. They are drawn into the section plan as straight lines and their border-curves are placed in the horizontal plan below the waterline plan. The centrelines are vital when actually building the hull. If they are fair, the seams are all right. Errors can be localised with the centrelines.

Section and waterline plans are of special importance when evaluating a yacht. They provide information about the yacht's cross-section and therefore about stability, draught and breadth. They also offer information about the boat's displacement and form resistance, which is important for the speed. The waterline plan offers details about the fullness of the boat's underwater hull and about the shape and size of keel and rudder etc. It also gives you an idea about the water flow around the hull.

Cylinder coefficient

At boat shows, dealers sometimes use the boat's low cylinder coefficient as a selling point. When dealing with cars, one nowadays talks about the low C_W-value, which the buyer cannot easily prove. It is similar to the hydrodynamic shape of a boat. A hydrodynamically favourable shape has always been obligatory for a yacht, although nobody knows the exact definition; today we try to give it a definition that comes pretty close to the cylinder coefficient.

We will give you a brief explanation so that you know what it is all about. Because shallow wave systems use less energy than steep ones at equal length, the fullness of the hull's ends (bow and stern) in relation to the midship section plays a vital role in the evaluation of a sailing yacht. The fullness influences the position and height of the waves and the dynamic buoyancy that is produced at the bottom of the hull. Both combined produce the wave resistance.

The cylinder coefficient describes the fullness of the hull, by dividing the overall resistance V through the length AM of the midship section multiplied by the LWL. The formula for the cylinder coefficient is therefore: V/AM x LWL. If it is applied to the speed-to-length ratio, the optimal values first produce a shallow curve and then a steep rising curve, as a criterion for the wave-producing resistance. The cylinder coefficient is between the value of 0.50 and 0.70, depending on the relative speed ($v_s/\sqrt{LWL}$) the boat was designed for. Heavy displacement yachts have narrow ends, which correspond to a low coefficient, while modern light displacement yachts, which achieve higher speeds on a broad reach or on a run, have fuller ends and therefore a higher coefficient. Pure fair-weather yachts that sail with slow speeds have a value of between 0.50 and 0.53. Cruisers with values between 0.53 and 0.55 have good

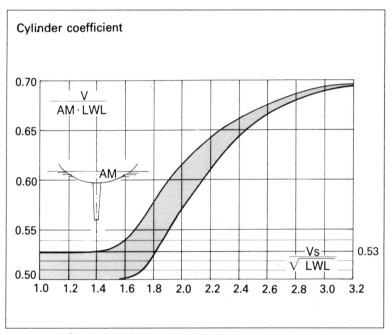

Fig 42 The cylinder coefficient tells you whether a yacht is narrow or beamy. The curve displays the optimal value depending on the speed-to-length ratio. Yachts with a value below 0.53 are therefore fair-weather yachts. Boats that are designed for stronger winds display a higher coefficient.

all-round qualities. Each speed has its corresponding cylinder coefficient: high values (up to 0.7) if the ends have a large displacement, as do light displacements with wide aft sections for planing. Unfortunately, the cylinder coefficient is not easily established, at least not at boat shows, but if some dealers use it for advertising they should at least state it in their brochure.

Index

Index

manoeuvrability, 28-32
  fin keel, 29
  long keel, 29
  short keel, 32
  turning circle, 97
  under engine, 102-3
mast profiles, 72-4
masthead rigs, 69-70
metacentric height, 103-6
midship section, 17, 49-51

pitching, 39, 40
propellers, 75-6
  stern gear, 75-6

ratios, 77-87
  length–beam, 78
  length–displacement, 81-3
  sail area-displacement, 83
  sail area-length, 83-5
  sailing speed-waterline, 85-7
resistance, 4-7
reverse drive, 102-3
rigging, 69-74
  angled crosstrees, 70-1
  cutter-rigs, 72
  fractional rigs, 70
  masthead rigs, 69-70
  mast profiles, 72-4
  two-masters, 72
rolling, 39, 40
rudders, 56-9

safety, 44-7
  static stability, 45-7
sail area, 20
  sail area–displacement ratio
    83
  sail area–length ratio, 83-5
  sail area–waterline ratio, 78-81
sailing speed–waterline ratio,
  85-7
sailing performance, 88-9, 74-100
  at a glance, 89-93
  by comparative values, 100
  diagram, 88-9
  heeling, 98-9

height to windward, 95-6
leeway, 98
on the water, 94-9
sailing to windward, 4, 25-8,
  97
speed, 94-5, 97
turning circle, 97
under sail, 88-91, 94-9
sailing to windward, 4, 25-8, 97
seaworthiness, 35-9
  accommodation, 36
skeg, 60-1
skin friction, 4
speed
  to windward, 97
  under sail, 94-5
stability, 9-12, 24, 103-7
  comparison, 106-7
  course stability, 28-32
  Dellenbough-coefficient,
    106-7
  fast sailing, 24
  heeling angle, 32-3, 104
  metacentric height, 103-6
  self righting, 103-4
  static, 45-7
  stiffness, 32-3
sterngear, 75
stern, shape of, 66-8
stiffness, 33
  heeling angle, 32-3
stopway, 103
symbols, 108-11

terms, 108-11
turning circle
  under sail, 97
  under engine, 102-3
two-masters, 72
type of boat, 13-15
waterline length (LWL), 17
  fast sailing, 23-4
wetted surface, 24
winged keel, 55

yawing, 39-40